The New Social Story™ Book

15th Anniversary Edition

By Carol Gray

Foreword by Dr. Barry Prizant
Author of *Uniquely Human: A Different Way of Seeing Autism*

New Sections!

★ Pre-school Children
★ Young Adults

REVISED & EXPANDED!

CREATIVE CHILD MAGAZINE
CREATIVE CHILD AWARDS
2017
BOOK
of the
Year Award
CREATIVECHILD.COM

Over 180 Social Stories™ That Teach Everyday Social Skills to Children and Young Adults with Autism or Asperger's Syndrome, and Their Peers

All marketing and publishing rights
guaranteed to and reserved by:

FUTURE HORIZONS
721 W. Abram Street
Arlington, TX 76013
Toll-free: 800-489-0727
Phone: 817-277-0727
Fax: 817-277-2270
Website: *www.FHautism.com*
E-mail: *info@FHautism.com*

Cover: Madison Coe with John Yacio III; Interior: Erin Stark (TLC Graphics) + John Yacio III (edits to the new edition)

Photos courtesy of *iStock.com* and *Dreamstime.com*

Publisher's Cataloging-In-Publication Data
(Prepared by The Donohue Group, Inc.)

Gray, Carol.
    The new social story book / by Carol Gray.—Rev. and exp. 15th Anniversary ed.

    p. : ill. ; cm.

    For printable forms: Purchase the PDF at www.fhautism.com.
    ISBN: 9781941765166

1. People with mental disabilities—Education. 2. Autistic children. 3. Developmentally disabled children. I. Title.
II Title: Social story book

LC4717.5 .N48 2010
371.92

Printed in the United States of America

This book is dedicated to Alex Gilpin,
in memory and celebration of his wonderful
and incredible life story.

■ ■ ■ ■

In Appreciation: The People of Social Stories™ History

I initiated the Social Story™ approach nearly twenty-five years ago. Since then, I have met thousands of wonderful, talented, interesting people. I am very impressed by the company that Social Stories™ keep. This book is the sum of their efforts, and I am grateful to each of them. Here, I'd like to describe the contributions of a few of them. I believe they are excellent representatives of the people—from all walks of life and all areas of Planet Earth—who write, read, or support Social Stories™—and add to their history each day.

Eric and Tim. Separated by fifteen years and 150 pounds difference in their silhouettes, Eric and Tim were both on my consultant caseload as the school year began in the fall of 1990. Eric was close to leaving his program at the high school; Tim was entering kindergarten. Eric and Tim never met, yet they each played an important role in Social Story™ history. A conversation with Eric caused me to see things from a far more accurate perspective; it was a paradigm shift. I was determined to put what I had learned from Eric into practice. One week later, I wrote the first Social Story™ for Tim. In my time, I've had many teachers; to date, however, Eric and Tim have been the most influential.

My husband, Brian. In the fall of 1990, I was having a lot of success writing stories for students on my caseload. To say I was hesitant to share that success with others is definitely an understatement. Despite my many protestations, which sprang from my innate shyness, my husband, Brian, encouraged me to share the success of Social Stories™ with others. The result was the first presentation on Social Stories™ in Indianapolis, Indiana. There was plenty of interest in my presentation, but I hid in my hotel room for the remainder of the conference. Two complete days of room service! Brian has been my coach—and, as always, my best friend—throughout the unique twists and turns of Social Story™ history.

Joanna Carnes and Barrett Gray. Brian and I are blessed with two incredible children, Joanna and Barrett. They definitely know—and are a big part of—Social Story™ history. Looking back, I'm impressed by their patient, calm support.

Joanna's maiden name is Gray, of course. She is now married to Mark, and they are the parents of our grandson, Ryan. Joanna may not realize this, but her comments have helped to bring this book to completion. At a critical point in the development of the manuscript, I was beyond overwhelmed; there were too many Stories, not enough minutes in the day—and too many other demands. Joanna listened to my frustration and, with a calm confidence that I will never, ever forget, she said, "You have to set some limits. Sometimes, you just have to say, 'That doesn't work for me right now.'" Suddenly, I saw them: the things that did not work alongside the goal of completing this project. I am very grateful to her, and I have been happily saying, "That doesn't work for me," (at the right times, of course) ever since. She's right. It works.

My son, Barrett, attended some of my earliest presentations. I remember one in particular, in Albuquerque. Barrett had the stack of evaluations in hand as we drove north from the conference. A hazy purple thunderstorm framed the horizon. Barrett was reading the comments on the evaluations to me. The majority of them were great, but it was the critical statements I took to heart. Praise didn't count. Barrett decided to throw the evaluations with negative comments into the back seat. Don't get me wrong—I value constructive criticism and feedback. But whenever I encounter criticism that I think is especially undeserved, in my mind I see a crumpled piece of paper, heading for the back seat, illuminated by flashes of lightning against a purple evening sky. Years later, over a glass of wine in a local bar, Barrett transformed the original Social Story™ ratio into the current Social Story™ Formula.

Joy Garand and Edna Smith, Ph.D. After the first presentation on Social Stories™ in Indianapolis, I met Joy Garand, a young special education teacher from Ohio, and Edna Smith, Ph.D, at the time Director of Missouri's Project ACCESS. Joy had attended my Indianapolis presentation, and she wrote to me a few months later to share her success with Social Stories™. I remember being surprised—not only did Social Stories™ work for me in Michigan, they were now working in Ohio, too! Joy and I co-authored the article, "Social Stories™: Improving the Responses of Students with Autism with Accurate Social Information," and Edna helped us submit it to the journal *Focus on Autistic Behavior*, where it was published in 1993. Meeting Joy and Edna led to the formal introduction of Social Stories™ to the field of autism.

Dr. Tony Attwood was one of the earliest professional supporters of Social Stories™. Tony contacted me for feedback on a portion of his new manuscript, titled, *Asperger's Syndrome: A Guide to Parents and Professionals.* He wanted to be sure that his description of Social Stories™ was accurate. Just as I had been surprised by Joy's success with Social Stories™, I was intrigued that a noted autism professional, from another country, was writing about my work. Not only that, but Tony genuinely understood Social Stories™. His description expanded my own understanding of them. (Today, Tony is a valued

The New Social Story™ Book, 15th Anniversary Edition
© by Carol Gray, Future Horizons, Inc.

friend of mine, and I deeply respect his contributions to our field. I was thrilled and honored when he agreed to write the Foreword to the 10th Anniversary Edition of this book.)

Peter Vermeulen, Ph.D., author of *Autism as Context Blindness* (2012), has expanded my thinking on the challenges that context presents to people with autism. In turn, his ideas are having an important impact on Social Stories. I have tremendous respect for his work. It's fun for me, too, to have him as a new friend.

Diane Twachtman-Cullen, Ph.D., CCC-SLP introduced me to *Wayne Gilpin,* President of Future Horizons. Diane encouraged Wayne to sit in on one of my earliest presentations. At first, I don't think Wayne believed that stories could have such a positive impact. I was impressed that he stayed and listened to my entire presentation that day … and changed his mind. Ultimately, he offered to print and distribute the very first book of Social Stories™, titled *The Original Social Story Book*—even though it had been turned down by several other publishers.

Keith Lovett, Director of Autism Independent (UK) brought Social Stories™ to the United Kingdom, and has sponsored Social Story™ workshops ever since. Keith is concerned for the education and welfare of people on the autism spectrum, and that includes protecting the quality of the instructional techniques that are used on their behalf. If Social Stories™ had a dad, it would be Keith. He looks out for the approach, informs me of any misinterpretations of it, and has steadfastly worked to ensure that high-quality Social Story™ workshops are held on his side of the Atlantic.

Team Social Stories™ (T.S.S.) and Social Stories Satellite Schools and Services (S.S.S.S.S.) Coaches work with me protect the integrity of Social Stories and conduct workshops. I remember when I was working for Jenison Public Schools, and I was talking with the personnel director. We were discussing the increasing number of my Social Story™ workshops and presentations. I asked, "How long can it possibly take to teach the world to write a Social Story™? This can't last forever." Now, I think it might. I am blessed to work with such a talented group of people. For information about T.S.S./S.S.S.S.S. go to CarolGraySocialStories.com.

My Cottage Friends are reflected in the pages of this book. They were the only "social norm" I had available to me, at our cottage, where most of the Stories in this book were written. I usually refer to them as the "cottage people," and they helped me research many of the Story topics. Often, I would ask them unusual questions about social concepts and skills. For example: What is the difference between a one- and a two-person hug? My questions led to discussions with little agreement, always framed by the unique personalities and unshakable mutual respect that defines this incredible group. I am indebted to them for their candid contributions to this book. I'd like to thank Paul and Pat, Granny, Jim and Maureen, Jeff and Marci, Sheri, Andy and C, Keith and Sandy, and Prudy and Jim. They make life on Planet Earth continually intriguing and interesting, easier, and a heck of a lot of fun. In my next life, I want to have them as my friends again.

Hank and Emma, my basset hounds, and my friends at Shaggy Pines Dog Park, in Ada, Michigan, played an important role in this second revision. At Shaggy Pines, friends are both canine and human, and randomly come and go to create a unique, un-orchestrated, and dynamic assortment of personalities and temperaments. We're not just walking and chasing balls there, we're sharing life's human and canine stories—from triumphs, to tragedies, and everything in between. Hank, Emma, and Shaggy Pines bring a clear and calm perspective to each and every day. Paws and people are better than chocolate.

The Boy at Barnes & Noble came up to me at a critical point during the first revision of this book. I wish I knew his name, so that I could thank him properly. Approaching the completion of the rough draft of the manuscript, I had been writing non-stop, eyes-open to eyes-shut, for over two weeks. I needed a change of writing venue, so I decided to head to the Rivertown Crossings Mall near our home. I worked on location. It was there that I wrote the Stories in this book about the up escalator and eating at a food court. I decided to head to Barnes & Noble, to write a Story about eating in a quiet bookstore café. However, the place was wall-to-wall people. I couldn't get to the café. So I sat down in an overstuffed chair, took out my laptop, and wrote the Story, "This Place is Busy!"

That's when he appeared: a boy about nine years old with curly brown hair. He was on his own—with his mother nearby—and approached me. Well, no, he approached my computer. He had many of the qualities of children on the autism spectrum. He read what I had written on the computer screen, looked up and around, and then turned to me and asked, "Does it help you to write a story about what is going on here?"

I was at a loss for an answer. I have it now. Yes, it does. Writing Stories about what is going on helps me because of the wonderful people, the incredible people, that it introduces me to. People like those whom I have listed here, people like the boy at Barnes & Noble, and people whom I have never met … but I know I would like if I did. Social Stories™ do keep the best company, and I have been—and will continue to be—honored to work alongside them.

Table of Contents

The New Social Story™ Book, 15th Anniversary Edition
© by Carol Gray, Future Horizons, Inc.

Foreword

What can be said in a foreword for a new revision of Social Stories™, an update of a classic already enshrined in the annals of autism history? I've been focused on supporting people with autism and developmental challenges for more than four decades, so I'm going to take advantage of my seniority and reflect on my experiences and the impact of Social Stories™ over many years.

Let's start with Carol, one of the most thoughtful, creative, and insightful educators to walk the earth (no exaggeration!!). I have had the privilege of presenting with Carol and hosting her as a conference speaker on numerous occasions. I am always in awe of her intuitive sense of how people with ASD experience the world that allows for a deep understanding of the types of knowledge and support that will be the most beneficial for them. Social Stories™ are but one of Carol's incredible innovations that have reshaped autism education and therapy; most importantly, it all happens on a foundation of the deepest love and respect she has for people she and others support. She values them as fellow humans sharing life together, an approach often sadly missing from educational and treatment efforts.

Social Stories™ are, hands down, the most widely used "focused intervention strategy" I have observed over my many years in autism research and consulting, and in programs with differing philosophies and approaches (e.g., behavioral as well as developmental). Social Stories™ are used by parents, siblings, professionals and para-educators of all shapes and sizes in school, home and community settings. If imitation is the sincerest form of flattery, the cup runneth over for Social Stories™. Social Stories™ have been copied, modified, and sometimes re-configured to such an extent that one must carefully scrutinize whether what one claims to be a Social Story™ actually meets Carol's specifically delineated specifications for structure and implementation. One of the most flagrant violations is when Social Stories™ are used primarily to correct behavior rather than enhance social understanding. Carol is so clear about this issue because she cares so much about the developing self-esteem of a person with developmental challenges. Of course, individualized support with a focus on building social understanding is a hallmark of Social Stories™.

The New Social Story™ Book, 15th Anniversary Edition
© by Carol Gray, Future Horizons, Inc.

Some practitioners think of Social Stories™ as simple. To the contrary, they are a strategy that is incredibly elegant when precisely formulated according to Carol's criteria. Social Stories™ have proven to be effective in educational practice and validated in research as an essential support for persons with developmental challenges and differences of all ages and a wide range of developmental abilities. In fact, in this latest revision, Carol has added two chapters of Stories for preschoolers (an entire one devoted to using the toilet), as well as expanding each chapter and adding a collection of Social Articles for adults.

Yes, Social Stories™ may be described as an effective and meaningful approach to support social understanding, but the ultimate and deeper goal is to empower children and older people by enhancing their understanding of social situations and social encounters in their lives, and thereby supporting their ability to be active participants in life's routines and activities. The effective use of Social Stories™ goes even further—it allows practitioners and parents to build trusting relationships through their support. Ultimately, the overarching goal of Social Stories™ is this: to help people to be self-determined, confident and competent individuals.

So now, dig in, enjoy and show the people you are teaching and supporting how much you love and care about them through your use of Social Stories™. Your efforts will help them thrive and live happily in this crazy world of ours.

BARRY M. PRIZANT, PH.D., CCC-SLP
Adjunct Professor
Artists and Scientists as Partners Group
Brown University

Director, Childhood Communication Services
Cranston, RI

Co-Developer, the SCERTS® Model
Author: *Uniquely Human: A Different Way of Seeing Autism*

How To Use This Book

I wrote this collection of Social Stories™ with you and the child or adolescent in your care (I refer to them as the "Audience" of your Stories) continually in mind. You may use the Stories in a variety of ways. They may be used directly from the book, or as a pattern to develop Stories of your own. This brief introduction will acquaint you with the resources in this book. For printable forms: Purchase the PDF at www.fhautism.com.

This book contains 185 Social Stories™ that I wrote either for students I was working with directly, or for fellow parents and educators. The Stories are divided into chapters according to their subject matter: Learning with Stories, Change, Mistakes, Me and My Feelings, Celebrations and Gifts, People Skills and Friendship, Bullying, Understanding Adults, Home and Community, School, and Planet Earth. Whereas some chapters focus on specific contexts, others focus on some of the most challenging issues facing children with autism spectrum disorders. I did my best to include the Stories most requested by parents and educators, and ones that I felt, from my personal experience, had helped children the most.

Some of the Stories in this book are designed to be used in groups, in sequence. As examples, the Fort Able Stories (#56-59) describe an imaginary comfort zone (Come to Fort Able=ComFortAble). Each Fort Able Story describes a "room" in a "fort." The bullying Stories (#95-102) are intended to be read/completed chronologically as well. You will discover other sets of sequenced Stories and related activities throughout the book.

For printable forms: Purchase the PDF at www.fhautism.com. All of the Stories are in Adobe PDF format, exactly as the Stories appear in this book. You can print Stories for individual use in the home, or include a Story in a classroom presentation to teach a skill to a group of students—and those are only a couple of examples. (Copyright permissions/restrictions are explained in detail on the PDF.)

Conversely, be aware that some students' reactions to the imagery can *negatively* impact their understanding of a social situation or skill. They may think that the Story applies to the child in the picture, but not to them. So if your child or student thinks very concretely, and has difficulty generalizing the skills, you may want to edit the story, customized with his or her experiences, and use the pre-illustrated Stories from the book for your reference only.

Note that Stories are editable in Adobe Acrobat if you own the full version of this program. If you have the free or Reader version of Adobe Acrobat, you will not be able to edit using this system. You may copy the story you want to edit, and paste it in Microsoft Word. Then you can edit the story to your liking. While most of the Stories can potentially be used as they are written, there are some Stories in this book that *have* to be revised before they are shared with your Audience. These are the Stories for a fictional character (e.g., Trevor, Mason, Fletcher) that include sample descriptions of past events. You will need to review those Stories for ideas, and then edit the corresponding file on the PDF, replacing existing details with your Audience's experiences. The individualized Story will make the most sense to your Audience if it is written from a first-person perspective, as though Audience is talking.

Many of the Stories in this book are intentionally "over-written." They include more text or longer sentences than I typically use when writing for students on my caseload. I did this to provide you with as many ideas and phrasing options as possible, while still maintaining sound Story structure. You, in turn, may review a Story and determine that it's ready to use with the person you are caring for. Or you may decide to revise it, in which case you should have enough text to shorten and/or personalize the Story as you see fit.

Stories may be easily shortened for younger or more severely challenged Audiences. In some cases, it may be possible to use the first sentence of each paragraph and delete the others. Other options to simplify a Story include omitting commas to create two separate sentences, or splitting one Story into two or more Stories.

Whether you are a beginner or an experienced author of Social Stories™, this book is designed to support your continued learning. The Social Story™ 10.2 Tutorials teach the art and science of developing a Social Story™. The tutorial section is your personal Social Story™ workshop to complete at your own pace. It includes an introduction to the tutorials, detailed descriptions of the 10.2 Social Story™ Criteria, and a practice activity for each criterion. Once you've completed the tutorials,, they are a handy reference to support your efforts in the months to come. I also encourage you to attend an official Social Stories™ training, where you can refine your Story writing and practice your skills with others.

The Internet is a wonderful resource. Unfortunately, much of the Social Story information online is outdated and inaccurate. Use caution. Many sites use the term Social Story without regard for its definition and emphasis on safety. They may use my name without my permission, making it seem as though I am in support of their information. Always look for the Social Story logo, which is a quality indicator. Trustworthy information is always available at CarolGraySocialStories.com and FHautism.com.

Thank you for your interest in Social Stories™. I am glad that this book has fallen into your good hands! Have fun exploring the Stories, completing the tutorials, and discovering the limitless uses of the PDF. I sincerely hope that this resource will come to your aid, like an old friend, when you need support, and become a trusted volume in your library for many years to come. Best wishes to you and your Audience!

Social Story™ 10.2 Tutorials

Introduction to the Social Story™ 10.2 Tutorials

Welcome to the Social Story™ 10.2 Tutorials, your introductory guide to developing Social Stories™ according to the current 10.2 criteria. This chapter will help you learn the basics of the approach so that you can begin to write Social Stories™ for those in your care. As you know, I wrote the Stories in this book for students with autism. I also wrote the Stories with you in mind as well, to introduce you to the art of writing Social Stories™. I will be referring to them frequently as you read and complete each tutorial.

As defined in the introduction to this book, A Social Story™ accurately describes a context, skill, achievement, or concept according to 10 defining criteria. These criteria guide Story research, development, and implementation to ensure an overall patient and supportive quality, and a format, "voice", content, and learning experience that is descriptive, meaningful, and physically, socially, and emotionally safe for the child, adolescent, or adult with autism. The criteria define what a Social Story™ is, and the process that researches, writes, and illustrates it.

In this chapter, the criteria are discussed in a series of ten tutorials. Work through them in sequence. Each tutorial opens with a brief definition of the criterion in italics, followed by a short discussion, activity and answers, and final notes. Answers are discussed in the text immediately following each activity. For this reason, complete each activity before reading further. It's also important to read the closing notes of each tutorial. They are not always a simple summary. As titled, they are final notes. They may contain information not previously mentioned, or suggest an additional exercise. Finally, it is not necessary to complete all of the tutorials in one session. In fact, it may be preferable to spread them out a bit, perhaps completing one each evening.

The 10.2 criteria are titled to make them easy to memorize. This makes it possible for Authors to develop a Social Story™ without having to run for this book each time.

The 10.2 criteria are:

1. One Goal
2. Two-Part Discovery
3. Three Parts and a Title
4. FOURmat Makes It Mine
5. Five Factors Impact Voice and Vocabulary
6. Six Questions Guide Story Development
7. Seven Is About Sentences
8. A Gr-eight Formula
9. Nine to Refine
10. Ten Guides to Implementation

After completing each tutorial, try to list the titles of the criteria that you have completed from memory. By the time you finish this chapter I am confident that you will have them memorized!

In this chapter, the 10 criteria are discussed in a series of tutorials. Work through them in sequence. Each tutorial opens with a brief definition of the criterion in italics, followed by a short discussion, activity and answers, and final notes. Answers are discussed in the text immediately following each activity. For this reason, complete each activity before reading further. It's also important to read the closing notes of each tutorial. They are not always a simple summary; as titled they are final notes and their content is varies. For example, the final notes of a tutorial may contain information not previously mentioned, or direct you to complete an additional activity. Finally, It is not necessary to complete all the tutorials in one session. In fact, it may be preferable to spread them out a bit, perhaps completing one each evening.

Relax and have fun as you learn to develop Social Stories according to the 10.2 criteria!

SOCIAL STORY™ VOCABULARY

First, it's important to establish some basic Social Story™ vocabulary. This vocabulary is designed to save us time so that Authors (that's you!) can efficiently focus on the task at hand:

- *Author:* The Author is you, the person who researches and develops a Social Story™. The Author may also be someone else, or a team of parents and professionals. Authors adhere to ten criteria that define each Social Story™ *and the process that creates it*. Due to their specialized skills, *Author* is always capitalized.

- *Audience:* The Author writes for a specific *Audience*. This is often a child, adolescent, or adult with autism. Each Social Story™ is developed with consideration of several individual factors, including but not limited to the age, gender, abilities, personality, preferences, and/or interests of the Audience. *Audience* is always capitalized when it is used in reference to Social Stories™.

- *Social Stories™:* The definition of Social Stories™ appears in the second paragraph of this introduction. Any time the term *Social Story™* is capitalized, it refers to a Social Story™ that meets all of the current 10.1 criteria. This distinguishes *Social Stories™* from "social stories" (lower case) that may not meet the criteria. When the term is used in these tutorials, it refers to Social Stories™ and Social Articles™. Social Articles are the more advanced counterpart of Social Stories™. They are often written for students who are older or academically more advanced. Social Articles adhere to the same criteria as Social Stories.

- *Story:* Any time the word *Story* is capitalized, I am referring to a Social Story™ that meets all the current criteria. This distinguishes Stories from stories (lower case) that may not meet the 10.2 criteria.

- *Team:* The Team includes parents and professionals, all those working together on behalf of an individual with ASD. Due to the specialized nature of this group, and the unique issues that they encounter and address, *Team* is always capitalized.

ACTIVITY

It is likely that you've already had some experiences with Social Stories™. Maybe you have read one, written one, heard about one, seen one, or been in a room with one. I've developed a short exercise for you. Is this a Social Story™? Complete the activity first and then continue reading.

Introduction Activity: Is This a Social Story™?

Directions: *Read the Story below. Is it a Social Story™?*   ❏ Yes ❏ No

Many people write Social Stories™. You may want to learn how to write Social Stories™, too. Then you will be able to write Stories for the students in your classroom. You'll have fun at the same time!

You may use the tutorials in this chapter to learn about the ten criteria that distinguish Social Stories™ from other visual strategies. Work through each tutorial at your own pace. Have fun!

Answer: This is not a Social Story™. It contains errors that deviate from the ten criteria. Here are three of them:

- Every Social Story™ has a title that represents the topic. In addition, Social Stories™ use sound story construction, using an introduction, body, and conclusion. This story does not have a title, and the delineation of an introduction, body, and conclusion is unclear.

- Social Stories™ contain only first and/or third person statements. Second person statements never appear in a Social Story. This story contains several second person statements.

- Social Stories™ are accurate and unassuming. Thus a phrase like, "You'll have fun at the same time," would not appear in a Social Story™. The phrase assumes the experience of the Audience; it is a guess that may or may not be true.

These are common errors. In my work, I have reviewed several stories that people refer to as "Social Stories™" that deviate from—or ignore altogether—many of the criteria. The term Social Stories™ is often used carelessly to refer to anything placed in writing for a person on the autism spectrum. As a result, there is a lot of misinformation that ultimately threatens the quality and safety of this important instructional tool.

To get a "feel" for this approach, randomly select a few Stories in this book. As you read them, note the title, introduction, body, and conclusion; the omission of second person statements, and the overall patient quality of each. The Stories in this book have additional characteristics in common as well. We'll be discussing each of their shared characteristics in the following ten tutorials.

FINAL NOTES

I want to personally thank you for taking the time to learn more about Social Stories™. You are also helping to preserve the integrity and quality of this approach worldwide. I sincerely appreciate your efforts. In return, I will do my best to support you as you work to learn the art of researching and writing Social Stories™.

The 1st Criterion: The Goal

DEFINITION

The Goal of a Social Story is to share accurate information using a content, format, and voice that is descriptive, meaningful, and physically, socially, and emotionally safe for the intended Audience.

ACTIVITY

Unlike the other tutorials, this one opens with an activity. Complete the activity. Then, read the rest of the tutorial.

Criterion 1 Activity: The Goal

Directions: *Reread the definition of the Goal. Answer this question:*

Is the Goal of a Social Story™ to get the Audience to do what we want him /her to do? Check one: ❑ Yes ❑ No

Answer: The most common misconception is that the goal of a Social Story™ is to change Audience behavior. This has never been the case. The Social Story™ Goal is to share accurate information meaningfully and safely. Admittedly, it is often behavior that draws attention to a specific concept, skill, or situation. However, if our objective is simply to change behavior, we are likely to focus on "telling the child what to do." Chances are the Audience has been told what to do—perhaps many times. Instead, our focus is on the underlying causes of frustration or misinformation. Authors work to identify and share information that supports more effective responses. The theory is that the improvement in behavior that is frequently credited to a Social Story™ is the result of improved understanding of events and expectations.

DISCUSSION

Every Social Story™ has an unfaltering respect for its Audience, regardless of the topic. Read the Story in this book titled, "Why People Take Baths or Showers." Many parents and professionals have difficulty helping the children, adolescents, or adults in their care understand the importance of personal hygiene. This Story addresses that topic with careful phrasing. Third person statements describe the importance of bathing in general, without pointing an accusing finger at the Audience. Also, the Story incorporates historical facts and a bit of humor to make the content interesting and fun. Other Stories in this book use similar strategies; all geared at sharing information accurately, respectfully, meaningfully, and safely.

The safety of a Story is an Author's first concern. In terms of physical safety, consider the following example. A mom writes a story for her son, Harrison, about swimming at the beach. She includes a photo of Harrison in the water. There is no one else in the photo. Dad was right next to the child when the photo was taken, although he was out of the range of the viewfinder. A typical child immediately interprets the photo in terms of its context, i.e. "That's when Dad and I were swimming together at the beach …" In contrast, from Harrison's perspective, the photo may give permission to swim alone, even though that is certainly not his mother's intent. To be discussed later, Authors of Social Stories™ work to develop text and illustration that is clear and accurate for the Audience. This supports meaningful comprehension of the Story and, as illustrated in this example, works to protect physical safety.

Social safety is equally important. Mrs. Barnes, a first grade teacher, writes a story for Adam, age six. She includes statements about her class: "We're all friends here. Friends cooperate with friends." Adam reads the story and goes out to recess. Two "friends" from his class approach him and tell him to pull down his pants. Working from the information in the story, that these two classmates are friends and friends cooperate with one another, Adam complies with their request. He's confused as they turn, laughing, and walk away. Adam's story was inaccurate. Classmates in a classroom are not all friends. Mrs. Barnes did not write a Social Story™. With all good and noble intentions, she wrote a socially unsafe story.

In my experience, the most frequent Author mistakes are statements in a story that threaten emotional safety. Here are some examples from the story archives: "I often interrupt;" "Sometimes, I hit other children;" and, "I often don't listen when people are talking to me, and that's rude." To be discussed in greater detail later when I describe the 5th criterion, self-depreciating statements, or negative references to the Audience, are not allowed in a Social Story™. They threaten self-esteem in the immediate sense, without providing the Audience with any information about alternative responses, and the rationale behind them. In addition, using the Audience voice—i.e. first person statements—in reference to negative behavior models the use of self-depreciating statements, and is at the same time, disrespectful of the Audience.

FINAL NOTES

The Goal is important to every Social Story™ and represents all of the remaining criteria. The 2nd, 3rd, and 4th criteria refer to the process of researching, developing, and implementing a Story with sound Story content, construction, and a meaningful format. The voice of every Story is defined by the 5th criteria, and is directly related to its characteristic patient and reassuring quality. The descriptive quality of every Social Story™ is the focus of the 6th, 7th, and 8th criteria. The 9th criterion requires Authors to check their work and seek feedback to ensure Story quality prior to implementation. Finally, the 10th criterion ensures that the process that carefully researches and develops every Story is reflected in its implementation. In the remaining Tutorials, each of these criteria will be discussed in more detail.

The 2nd Criterion:
Two-Step Discovery

DEFINITION

Keeping the Goal in mind, Authors gather relevant information to 1) improve their understanding of the Audience in relation to a situation, skill, or concept, and/or 2) identify the specific topic(s) and type(s) of information to share in the Story.

DISCUSSION

There are two parts to this criterion, both rooted in Story information. First, Authors gather information to (ideally) discover a specific Social Story™ topic or an alternate solution. (Sometimes, in the process of gathering information an Author discovers a solution that does not require a Social Story™.) Information in hand a Story topic is identified.

The 2nd Criterion is frequently dismissed or overlooked. Many Authors fail to realize how this criterion can make the difference between an ineffective story and one that "hits the nail on the head." Among the ten criteria, this is the "lead domino" that contributes to Story quality early in the writing process. It has a direct impact on an Author's subsequent efforts.

GATHER INFORMATION

The original rationale for Social Stories™—now increasingly supported by first-hand accounts and research—is that a child or adult with autism may frequently perceive daily experiences differently.

This requires Authors to "abandon all assumptions". Authors consider how a situation may look, feel, smell, or sound like to the Audience, or how a concept may be perceived, understood, and/or processed. The objective is to use any and every source of information that will improve understanding of the Audience in relation to the general topic area.

It is important to gather information before identifying a specific topic. Authors begin with a general targeted situation or topic area, gather information, and then discover the specific topic and Story focus within it. Getting the sequence right on this one –gathering information first prior to identification of a specific topic or title—saves Author time and Audience frustration.

There are several sources of information. Of course, some of them are more relevant in some cases than others. It's important to consult with others who have knowledge or experience with the Audience and/or the general topic or situation. Regardless of the topic or circumstances, Authors must consult with parents or caregivers prior to developing a story. Parents and caregivers have a rare expertise, a long-term relationship with the Audience and varied and numerous experiences. The bottom line is that they know the Audience better than anyone, providing insights that others may overlook, as well as unique details. Their input often brings a Story project into sharp focus.

Observation is also an important source of information. At least two observations are required. The first is from a third-person "fly on the wall" perspective to gather information about the relevant cues that define a situation or concept. The second observation places the Author in the middle of the action where the situation or concept is continually considered in terms of Audience perception, cognition, personality, and his/her previous experience.

In addition to Team consultation and observation, there are many other possible sources of information. For example, an Author may record objective data to understand a puzzling Audience response. An Internet search may yield helpful information. In my office I have a set of fifteen dictionaries geared to a variety of ages and abilities. I don't need to spend time groping for the right word, or how to describe the meaning of a given term to my Audience. They are invaluable in helping me as I define the topic and throughout the process of writing the story.

IDENTIFYING A SPECIFIC TOPIC

A topic is often discovered as information is collected. This is called topic discovery and is preferable to an Author's best guesses. When a topic is discovered, the roots of Audience confusion, misinformation, or challenge become readily apparent and the specific topic is obvious. In contrast, best guess topics—while based upon the information that has been gathered—are a hit-or-miss speculation. For example, Andrew, a student in Mrs. Clark's first grade class, struggled in math. Only once had he raised his hand for help. I was curious as to why Andrew had given up on the hand-raising process. I decided to try drawing a picture with Andrew to learn more. We drew about what happened when he had raised his hand on that one occasion. While doing so, Andrew said, "I'm never going to raise my hand again. My teacher doesn't know anything about math." I asked why he felt that way. "Well, I raised my hand. Mrs. Clark came over and said, 'OK Andrew, what's the first number?' Mrs. Gray, she doesn't even know her numbers!" The Story topics became clear. I wrote two of them. One described what his teacher knows. It included copies of her diploma and first grade math assignments that she completed. The second Story explained why teachers ask questions when they already know the answers. Immediately after reading both Stories, Andrew began raising his hand once again. Discovered topics are great. In my experience they tailor Author efforts early in the story process and result in Stories that are often immediately effective.

A final important note about topics: Fifty percent (50%) of all Social Stories™ must applaud what the Audience is doing well. In this book, the Story, "Using 'Excuse Me' to move through a crowd" is an example. The rationale is simple. Given that Social Stories™ are helpful in teaching new concepts and skills, they may also be just as powerful in adding meaning and detail to praise. What a wonderful way to build self-esteem! The same criteria apply to Stories that praise, as they do to other Stories, including the requirement to gather information. If Authors only write stories that describe challenging situations, concepts, or skills, they are ignoring an important and required part of the writing process. They are not writing Social Stories™.

The New Social Story™ Book, 15th Anniversary Edition
© by Carol Gray, Future Horizons, Inc.

ACTIVITY

Criterion 2 Activity: Two-Step Discovery

Directions: *Read each passage below. Is it TRUE (T) or FALSE (F)?*

1. A Story topic is like a sewing pattern. When writing a Social Story, start with the topic.

    T   F

2. Some Social Story topics are discovered; others are an Author's "best guess."

    T   F

3. In the process of gathering information for a Social Story, an Author may discover an alternate solution where no Story is needed.

    T   F

Answer: Two-Step Discovery underscores the importance of carefully gathering quality information prior to identification of a topic, which makes the first statement FALSE. The second statement is TRUE. While we would love to be able to discover the very best Story topic each and every time, Authors often have to sit down, review the information that they have gathered, and make the best guess. The final statement is TRUE. Authors may discover the nature of a problem or concern and its counterpart solution simultaneously. No Story required.

FINAL NOTES

Compared to many of the other Social Story Criteria, the 2nd Criterion is a relative newcomer. It was introduced in 2010 when the original ten Social Story Criteria (Social Stories 10.0) were revised and reorganized to include the processes that create and implement each Story document. In the short time since its introduction, it has quickly gained prominence and detail. This is because it represents a critical first step that is all too often a missed or miss-step. In each Social Story 10.2 workshop there is a quote that aptly summarizes the role and contribution of the 2nd Criterion: *Get this right and the Story will almost write itself.*

The 3rd Criterion: Three Parts and a Title

DEFINITION

A Social Story/Article has a title and introduction that clearly identifies the topic, a body that adds detail, and a conclusion that reinforces and summarizes the information.

DISCUSSION

Similar to all good stories, Social Stories™ have roots in sound structure and organization: a title and introduction; a body; and a conclusion. When we recognize the purpose of a Social Story™ and its unique Audience, these "story basics" take on increased importance. Select two or three Stories in this book to review, and note how each includes these important story elements.

Writing with the introduction, body, and conclusion in mind helps Authors efficiently identify (introduction), describe (body), and reinforce (conclusion) the most important concepts in a Social Story™. The introduction focuses attention on the first challenge: clearly stating the topic. A single sentence may complete the task: "If I lose a toy, people can help." Sometimes, we may recruit the child's attention first, "My name is Jeremy," and then announce the topic. The body immediately follows the introduction, adding further description and/or explanation with statements like, "Mom or Dad knows how to find my toy. We will try to think and look." The conclusion refers us back to the beginning—the concepts, situations, and/or achievements that initiated the Story. It restates the original purpose with the benefit of additional information, "People can help me look for my toy." Collectively, the introduction, body, and conclusion guide the development of Social Stories™ regardless of their complexity or length.

The New Social Story™ Book, 15th Anniversary Edition
© by Carol Gray, Future Horizons, Inc.

In addition to organizing and sequencing our thoughts while writing a Story, the structure provided by the title, introduction, body, and conclusion clarifies information for our Audience. For any child, knowing what a Story is about first (the title and introduction) provides a frame where all subsequent details (the body) can be placed. As the Story draws to a close, important details can be reinforced and in some cases, personalized to the child's experience (the conclusion). The same is true of Social Stories™, with one difference. The Audience has an inherent difficulty conceptualizing, sequencing, "getting the gist" or the bigger picture, and applying information to their own experience. This increases the critical role of clear organization within each Story.

ACTIVITY

Answer: In order to have a clear and meaningful introduction, body, and conclusion, a Social Story™ has a minimum of three sentences ... The title, of course, doesn't count.

FINAL NOTES

Before moving on stop a moment and try to recite the first three criteria. Yes, now—before reading a word further. They are: One Goal, Two-Part Discovery, and Three Parts and a Title. To this point, we've discussed the Goal, and explored what is meant by Two-Step Discovery. We've also covered basic story structure, and why every Social Story™ has Three Parts & a Title. "FOURmat Makes it Mine!" is next!

Criterion 3 Activity: Three Parts and a Title

Directions: *Considering the 3rd Criterion, complete the sentence below:*

A Social Story™ must have a minimum of _____ sentences.

THE 4th CRITERION: FOURmat Makes It Mine!

DEFINITION

The Social Story™ format is tailored to the individual abilities, attention span, learning style and—whenever possible—talents and/or interests of its Audience.

DISCUSSION

In a Social Story™, format refers to the individualization, organization and presentation of text and illustration. There are several ways to tailor text and illustration to the needs of the Audience. Several individualized factors are considered, including the length of the Story, sentence structure, vocabulary, font and font size, tailoring to Audience talents and/or interests, and the organization of the text and illustration. The art and science of every Social Story™ is selecting format elements that are most likely to be meaningful for the Audience. In other words, format is developed from an understanding of the Audience, so that in turn it may help the Audience understand.

AGE AND ABILITY

The age and ability of an Audience is central to Story format. For a younger child, the time required to peruse each page—or an entire Story—needs to be brief! Generally, a Social Story™ for a young child will contain 3-12 short sentences. In addition, eliminating commas to create two or more shorter sentences is recommended. This matches the duration of many of their other interactions and activities throughout the day. Shorter Stories are challenging to write. A struggle often ensues between the opposing goals of covering the topic and keeping the Story brief. A good solution is to "write everything down" first, then edit the text back to the desired length.

Sometimes, a topic will be impossible to cover in a short Story. To meet the demands of the topic and respect the attention of the child, information can be broken down into two or more shorter Stories. Called Social Story Sets, this format limits the length of each Story while making it possible to include important details and link concepts.

Longer Stories are often more suitable for older or more advanced Audiences. These Stories will contain twelve sentences or more—up to and including extensive Social Articles. Considering the unique and complex topics that often accompany increased age and skill, having more time to explain the "ins and outs" that are involved is a welcome and necessary freedom! In this case "25 words or less" isn't desirable or necessary; covering the topic takes a higher priority.

REPETITION, RHYTHM, AND RHYME

Repetition, rhythm, and rhyme may be an excellent match for an Audience who thrives on routines and predictability. These elements can hold attention as well as infuse familiarity into a new or difficult topic. For these reasons, many Social Stories™ use rhythmic and repetitive phrasing: "On the playground, I may play on the swings, I may play on the slide, I may play on the monkey bars, or I may play with something else." Rhyme is often overlooked as Stories are developed, despite the important role that it can play. Rhyme does not have to be used throughout a Story to be effective; it may be used to emphasize just one idea. For example, "Feeling angry is okay; it's important what I do and say." Despite the potential benefits of incorporating repetition, rhythm, and/or rhyme into a Story, it's important to consider Audience preference as well. Some Audiences may regard these elements as "babyish," and thus insulting. This brings up an important rule of thumb: Never risk insulting the Audience.

TALENTS AND INTERESTS

As readers, we all choose to read those books that are in line with our interests and abilities. Few of us want to read information that is very difficult or hard to understand. It's frustrating, uninteresting, and ... it puts us to sleep. It's important for Authors to keep in mind that "social" is their most frequent topic, and it is a topic that is exceedingly difficult for the Audience. For this reason, anything that the Authors can do to make the information interesting and fun increases the likelihood that a Story will be effective.

Many of the other Criteria ensure that information is individualized to Audience needs and ability. The 4th Criterion personalizes a Story with consideration of Audience experiences, important relation-ships, interests, and preferences in the development of content, text, illustration, and format. Also included are highly creative elements that reflect—and in some cases demonstrate—story content. These increase Audience enthusiasm for a Story as well as comprehension and potential ownership of concepts and information. The inclusion of these will also increase the likelihood for generalization of concepts and skills.

It is the consideration of Audience talents and interests that often results in memorable 'museum quality' Stories. One grandmother embroidered a Social Story™ about what love means on a quilt for her grandson's bed. A mother pasted a Social Story™ about buying new shoes on the top of a shoe box, placing photos of the exact shoes her child would try on in the box (taken the day before with a digital camera and the store manager's permission). For a child with an interest in the United States Postal System, Stories arrived via the mail, in interesting containers with postmarks from new locations. One teacher cuts the pages of every Story into a representative shape, for example, a Story about lunch cut in the shape of a lunch box. Frustrated by the behavior of an entire classroom, a music teacher wrote a Story that identified the rules, and then set it to music to open each lesson. Hopefully, these ideas will inspire you about the potential for building additional meaning and fun into Social Stories™.

In terms of creativity, careful consideration is the rule. Be cautious with creativity; never sacrifice Story meaning or safety for an over-the-top idea. What seems fun and cute may be confusing or even fright-ening to a specific Audience. Think of the Audience and how the idea may be perceived or understood. If it's risky, don't do it.

On the positive side, creativity with cautious restraint results in Stories that captivate the Audience and promote learning. With a balance of creativity and caution, the 4th Criterion can be the difference between a story that is read by the Audience and tossed aside, and a Social Story™ that is taken to bed.

The New Social Story™ Book, 15th Anniversary Edition
© by Carol Gray, Future Horizons, Inc.

ILLUSTRATION

Illustration plays a critical role in many Social Stories™. For our purposes here, illustration refers to the use of visual arts to support the meaning of text. Illustration options include but are not limited to: actual objects; photos; video; drawings; PowerPoint®; figures; charts; and diagrams. The most effective illustrations highlight and summarize information, captivate interest, and improve Audience comprehension.

Authors are as cautious with illustration as they are with text. They look for anything that may mislead or confuse the Audience. If a child makes frequent literal interpretations of words and statements, he/she may do the same with illustrations. For example, Thomas has a toileting Story. It contains plenty of eye-catching color and detail. Throughout the story, Thomas wears a crayon-yellow shirt and bright blue pants. In the Story, the bathroom has two small, symmetrical windows. Thomas concludes with some relief that should he ever get a yellow shirt and find himself in a bathroom with two small symmetrical windows, he may be asked to try to use the toilet. Imagine his distress with those who ask him to use a toilet without those factors in place! Thomas' literal interpretations of illustrations will not be an issue for all children. For Thomas, though, minimizing the use of color or extensive detail in the illustrations may reduce the likelihood of misinterpretation.

Photographs are often used to illustrate a Social Story™. The benefit of photographs is that 1) they may hold meaning for a child where drawings have failed, 2) they are accurate, and 3) they are fast and easy to create, particularly if digital cameras are used. However, a photo may be too accurate. The Audience may assign irrelevant meaning to extraneous detail. Photographs work best when the subject is clear, and the background is free of competing detail. Black and white photographs may be helpful, as they contain interesting subject details and minimize extraneous factors (color, for example). In addition, circling important details on a photograph can help to focus Audience participation on the most relevant aspects of an illustration.

Several factors determine the selection of illustrations for a Social Story™. Similar to choosing effective and meaningful text, it is equally important to match illustrations to a child's ability and interests. For example:

1. Does the Audience have the prerequisite skills to use this form of illustration?

2. Will the Audience understand the representational meaning of a simple drawing?

3. Would a chart or a graph "work harder" with this content, and would the Audience understand its meaning?

4. Has the Audience previously demonstrated interest in this type of illustration?

5. Has this method of illustration captured this child's attention in the past?

6. Would a combination of two or more forms of illustration work best with this Audience?

When Authors keep several illustration options in mind and consider the questions listed above; they will be able to select a method of illustration that will match the learning profile of the Audience.

ACTIVITY

Criterion 4 Activity: FOURmat Makes It Mine!

Select a Story from this book for someone you know. Using the individual factors listed in the discussion of this criterion as a guide (age and ability repetition, rhythm, and rhyme; talents and interests; and illustration preferences), list ideas to tailor the text and illustration to your Audience.

FINAL NOTES

The 4th Criterion of the Social Story™ 10.2 Criteria is like Texas in the United States. It's big. There are many possible format factors and variations, countless ways that an Author can improve the odds of effectively reaching the Audience. Creative Authors will discover as they translate each new topic into a meaningful format that despite the required adherence to 10 criteria, writing Social Stories™ holds unlimited possibilities. The best Authors understand this potential and discover something new about the approach with every Story that they write.

The 5th Criterion: Five Factors Define Voice and Vocabulary

DEFINITION

A Social Story™ has a patient and supportive voice and vocabulary that is defined by five factors. They are:

1. *1st or 3rd person perspective;*

2. *Positive & patient tone;*

3. *Past, present, or future tense;*

4. *Literally accurate; and*

5. *Accurate meaning.*

DISCUSSION

The 4th Criterion tailors Story format to the Audience. The 5th Criterion gives additional detail and picks up where the 4th Criterion leaves off with five factors to define Story voice and vocabulary. Working together, these factors result in the characteristic safe, patient and reassuring quality that distinguish Social Stories™ from social scripts and other similar visual strategies.

1. FIRST- OR THIRD-PERSON PERSPECTIVE STATEMENTS

Selecting an effective perspective from which to share the information in a Social Story™ is important, and pre-requisite to placing any words on paper. A few factors impact this decision and ultimately determine the Story's voice.

Many Social Stories™ are written in a first person voice, as though the Audience is describing the situation, event, or concept. Writing from this perspective, a Story will often contain both first and third person sentences. Presenting information from an Audience vantage point increases Author responsibility. Authors take extra care to make sure that they do not "put words into the mouth" of the Audience, or presume to make an uninformed guess regarding the Audience perspective of the situation. For example, statements like, "I will like eating lunch at recess," are presumptuous, potentially inaccurate, and unsuitable for placement in a Social Story™.

Many Social Stories™ are written exclusively from a third-person voice, similar to an article. Referred to as a Social Articles, they are suitable for older or more advanced children, adolescents, or adults. Social Articles often incorporate format elements from newspapers, using columns, advanced vocabulary, and/or Times New Roman font to minimize any "babyish" or insulting quality in the format or text.

2. POSITIVE AND PATIENT TONE

A Social Story™ uses positive language. This is very important in descriptions of behaviors, especially those that are typical or desirable in a given situation. A person with autism is likely to be challenged, corrected, and re-directed more than his or her peers. By clearly describing desirable responses and the rationale behind them, Authors patiently share ideas about what to do in a given situation.

Social Stories™ safeguard the self-esteem of the Audience. Authors never use the Audience voice in reference to his or her negative behavior. As examples, sentences like, "I have difficulty listening to my teacher," or "Sometimes when I am angry, I hit people," provide little usable information and never appear in a Social Story™. Instead, an Author may describe a specific negative behavior in general, without pointing a finger specifically at the Audience. In addition, information about learning more effective responses is also included. For example, an Author may write, "All children have difficulty with interrupting at times. With practice, they learn when to talk and when to listen." This maintains a positive tone, even in light of a negative topic. It helps to build and preserve a child's positive self-esteem, while sharing what may be new social information.

3. PAST, PRESENT, AND/OR FUTURE TENSE

People readily use information from their past to complete a current task, anticipate likely outcomes, and problem solve. A Social Story that describes the connections between life's experiences adds a meaningful dimension to the topic. In Chapter 1, the Story, "Learning with Stories," describes three experiences of the Audience. Here's one of them: "Once, my mom was teaching me to tie my shoes. She told me a story about how her grandfather taught her to tie shoes. I tried it, practiced it, and learned how to tie my shoes." Even the simplest of Stories can point out connections between related events and highlight the ties that are critical to learning and navigating through each day.

4. LITERAL ACCURACY

Social Story Authors select words, phrases, and sentences that are accurate, even if interpreted literally. Many people with autism make "face value" assessments of phrases and statements, without the additional meaning that social insight provides. For this reason, a Social Story™ contains the most absolutely sincere language possible, where there is no difference between intended and stated meanings. If the intended meaning of a word or phrase changes if it is interpreted literally, it is not used. The only exception to the requirement of literal accuracy relates to the use of metaphors and analogies. Metaphors and analogies may be used in a Social Story™ if they are meaningful for the specific Audience. Outside of analogies and metaphors, a Social Story™ is a sincere and accurate description of the topic.

5. ACCURATE VOCABULARY

Social Story™ Authors use the most efficient vocabulary possible by selecting words most likely to be clear messengers of their meaning. Two considerations apply. The first is related to the use of positive language. Positive verbs are preferable to their negated counterparts. For example, instead of: "I will try not to run in the hallway," it's better to use: "I will try to walk in the hallway." A negated verb only describes what not to do, not what is preferable or expected. There is also a risk with some Audiences that 'don't run' may be interpreted as 'run'. Second, verbs are notorious for the subtle but critical contrasts between them. Consider the difference between, "Dad will get the milk at the store," and "Dad will buy milk at the store." People who get milk may be shoplifting. We want Dad to buy the milk!

An Audience may demonstrate strong emotional reactions to specific words. For example, words like "change", "new", or "different" may be associated with negative situations, causing the Audience to feel uncomfortable or uneasy. The use of alternative vocabulary helps to keep Audience attention relaxed and focused on the topic at hand. Instead of the word, "new", for example, "another" may be used. Though the use of alternative vocabulary is a consideration, and may not be necessary for all Audiences.

ACTIVITY

The 5th Criterion includes several writing considerations:

1. Exclusive use of first and/or third person statements (with omission of all second person statements);

2. Maintenance of an overall positive and patient tone, regardless of topic;

3. Consideration of the potential value of present tense information, as well as relevant experiences or future implications to enhance meaning, build self-esteem, and/or support generalization;

4. Literal accuracy to help to ensure accurate meaning; and

5. Selection of the most accurate and comfortable vocabulary for the Audience.

To complete the following activity, consider all the above factors simultaneously to determine the sentences that are AOK—as well as those that would never be used—in a Social Story™.

Criterion 5 Activity:
Five Factors Define Voice and Vocabulary

Directions: *Which of the sentences may be used in a Social Story™? Place a "Y" for "YES!" and an "N" for "NEVER."*

1. _____ I shouldn't run in the house.

2. _____ I will keep the paint on the paper.

3. _____ You'll have fun at recess.

4. _____ Veterinarians know a lot about dogs, cats, and other animals.

5. _____ This is no time to decide on an itinerary because our plans are up in the air.

Answer: There is one sentence we can save for use in a Social Story™, and that is #4. All the others, as written, are unacceptable. Here's how each of them could be revised for a Social Story:

1. Many times, it's important to walk in the house.

2. I will try to keep the paint on the paper.

3. At recess, I have a choice. I may play on the swings. I may play with the ball. Or, I may decide to play something else.

4. MISSING

5. When Dad knows the dates for his vacation this year, our family will plan a trip to California.

FINAL NOTES

The 5th Criterion guides how words are used in a Social Story. It determines Story voice, tone, related relevant content, and clear and meaningful vocabulary. It is put to work within the frame provided by all of the previous Criteria, as it adds detail to Author efforts to write effective Stories.

The New Social Story™ Book, 15th Anniversary Edition
© by Carol Gray, Future Horizons, Inc.

The 6th Criterion: Six Questions Guide Story Development

DEFINITION

A Social Story answers relevant "wh' questions, describing the context (where), time-related information (when), relevant people (who), important cues (what) basic activities, behaviors, or statements (how) and the reasons or rationale behind them (why).

DISCUSSION

The basic "wh" questions (who, what, when, where, why, and how) are important to developing an outline to guide Author efforts to create a meaningful Story for the Audience. They remind us to include basic information that we may otherwise take for granted, where and when the situation occurs, who is involved, how events are sequenced, and what occurs. Next, other "obvious" details are considered. What cues or concepts may the Audience have missed? Often, this is also the answer to the last "wh" question, why.

At face value, looking to "wh" questions to describe the basic features of a situation or concept seems quite simple. Occasionally, this is where our greatest challenge may lie; especially in terms of why. One of my first Social Stories™ was developed for a kindergarten student to describe "lining up" at school. I had to think - why is it so important to have children stand and walk in lines? If I couldn't come up with the rationale, how could we support the practice? A few moments later, the assumed rationale became apparent. Basically, lining up is the safest way to move children from one part of a school to another.

Rest assured that thousands of Social Stories™ and many years later, only once have I been at a loss to figure out why. It was for a Story to describe a child's kindergarten routine. I couldn't make sense of the eight adults and seven locations that were to be part of his daily routine! What was I to write? Sometimes, adults design overwhelming programs for innocent children. This is okay. Unable to describe in good conscience his schedule, I abandoned writing the Story in favor of making the needed changes in his school day. The process of answering "wh" questions, coupled with the collective accuracy and sincerity required by the other guidelines, renders it impossible to write a Social Story™ to describe or "sell" an unwise idea, strategy, or plan.

A Story can answer "wh" questions very efficiently. For example, a single, opening sentence can answer many "wh" questions: My family (who) is going (what) to the beach (where) today (when). This may be followed with a brief statement that answers how the trip to the beach will occur: We'll ride in our car to the beach, or a sentence that explains why this activity is planned: Many families have fun when they visit the beach. In this way, a Social Story™ succinctly identifies who is involved, where and when a situation occurs, what is happening, how it happens, and why. Before writing the first sentence, another who must be considered: whose voice tells the Story?

ACTIVITY

Criterion 6 Activity:
Six Questions Guide Story Development

Directions: *Read the Story in this book, "Absent Today? This is okay!"*

Which "wh" questions are answered in this Story?

Answer: There are several "wh" questions that are answered in this Story. Here are a few of them:

- Who is absent from school?

- What did my parents say about being absent?

- When will I be back in school?

- Where do sick children need to be?

- Why are students sometimes absent from school?

- How will I get my assignments?

The questions listed in your answer may vary from those above. This is okay! As mentioned early, a single statement in a Social Story™ may hold the answers to several questions.

FINAL NOTES

Thank goodness for "wh" questions! They can save Authors from staring at a computer screen or blank piece of paper. When an Author is at a loss for where to begin, how to get started, or what to write, thinking of relevant "wh" questions provides a quick rescue. The answers to those questions provide clarity and meaning for the Audience.

The 7th Criterion: Seven is About Sentences

DEFINITION

A Social Story™ is comprised of Descriptive Sentences, and may also have one or more Coaching Sentence(s). Sentences adhere to all applicable Social Story™ Criteria.

DISCUSSION

Descriptive Sentences

Let's start with the definition of Descriptive Sentences: Descriptive Sentences accurately describe relevant aspects of context, including external and/or internal factors while adhering to all applicable Social Story™ Criteria. They are free of assumption or bias, judgment, devaluation, and/or unidentified opinion.

Descriptive Sentences are trustworthy carriers of information. Descriptive Sentences describe observable external factors related to a topic, including those that are not as readily apparent (relevant thoughts, feelings, cultural expectations, etc.). As an example, what follows are two Descriptive Sentences. The first describes observable information and the second shares a related cultural value:

People shop for food in a grocery store. Buying healthy food is a smart choice.

Descriptive Sentences often describe or refer to another person's (or group of people) internal state, including and not limited to knowledge, thoughts, feelings, beliefs, opinions, motivation, health, illness, personality, etc.

The following Descriptive Sentence is about what a grocery store cashier knows:

Cashiers know how to help customers pay for their groceries.

Descriptive Sentences may also be used to enhance the meaning of surrounding statements by describing commonly shared beliefs, values, or traditions within a given culture. Consider this example:

When I am riding in the car, I will try to keep my seat belt fastened. This is very, very, very important for safety.

The second sentence enhances the meaning of the first—it is a Descriptive Sentence that reinforces the meaning or importance of the sentences that surround it. The first sentence is a Coaching Sentence, to be discussed next.

Coaching Sentences

A Coaching Sentences are defined as: Coaching Sentences gently guide behavior

via descriptions of effective Team or Audience responses, or structured

Audience Self-Coaching, adhering to all other applicable Social Story Criteria.

There are three kinds of Coaching Sentences.

1. Sentences that Coach the Audience describe expected or effective responses or possible choices, as in: When we have free time, I may draw, read, or maybe choose another quiet activity.

2. Sentences that Coach the Team provide suggestions or reminders for caregivers, things they can do to support the Audience. Here's an example: My mom will show me how to load and start the dishwasher.

3. Sometimes the Audience writes their own Coaching Sentence. Referred to as Self-Coaching Sentences, the Audience reviews the Story with a parent or caregiver, and writes a sentence of his own to contribute to the Story. Here's an example: When the teacher says, "Eyes and ears at the front of the room," I will try to remember that it means to listen to what the teacher says and watch what he is doing. Self-Coaching Sentences aid in Audience ownership and recall of a Story, as well as generalization of Story content across time and place.

ACTIVITY

Criterion 7 Activity:
Seven is About Sentences

Directions: *What type of sentence is it? Indicate Descriptive (D) or Coaching (C).*

1. Many students in my group have ideas about our project. _____

2. I will try to listen to the ideas of others in my group. _____

3. Many children want to be first in line. _____

4. I will try to stay calm when another child is first in line. _____

5. Learning to drive requires some practice. _____

Answer: 1. D   2. C   3. D   4. C   5. D

There are three Descriptive and two Coaching Sentences. "Many students in my group have ideas about our project" is a general description of the thoughts of other classmates. "I will try to listen to the ideas of others in my group" coaches the Audience. "Many children want to be first in line" describes a common desire among young children. "I will try to stay calm when another child is first in line" is a sentence that Coaches the Audience. "Learning to drive requires some practice" is a Descriptive Sentence about how people learn to drive.

FINAL NOTES

It is important to be able to identify Descriptive and Coaching Sentences and to understand the role that each plays. For additional practice, select any Story in this book, read each sentence, and then stop and decide if it is a Descriptive or Coaching Sentence. Or, select a topic of your own and write a Descriptive Sentence for it. Creating activities of your own, of course, is not limited to this Criterion. Feel free to create your own additional practice or review for any Criterion.

The New Social Story™ Book, 15th Anniversary Edition
© by Carol Gray, Future Horizons, Inc.

The 8th Criterion:
A GR-EIGHT Formula!

DEFINITION

One Formula ensures that every Social Story describes™ more than directs.

DISCUSSION

The Social Story™ Formula is an equation that defines the relationship between the Descriptive and Coaching Sentences in a Social Story™. It guarantees that every Story focuses on describing inter-actions or events, and that it also includes, where applicable, an explanation of the rationale that underlies what people think, say, or do. The Formula provides for an unlimited number of Descriptive Sentences in a Social Story™. At the same time, the Formula limits the number of Coaching Sentences (Figure 1).

Figure 1: The Social Story™ Formula

$$\frac{\text{DESCRIBE (Total number of Descriptive Sentences in the story)}}{\text{COACH (Total number of Sentences that Coach in the story)}} \geq 2$$

To use the formula, an Author counts the number of each type of sentence, adds their totals, and then divides the total number of sentences that DESCRIBE by the total number of sentences that COACH. To be considered a Social Story™, the answer must always be greater than or equal to two. If there are no Coaching Sentences, "1" is used as the divisor.

The quotient in the formula is referred to as the Social Story™ Rating. A very descriptive Story will have a Rating that is almost equal to the total number of Descriptive Sentences. A Story that is more directive, that contains more Coaching Sentences, will have a Rating that is closer to - but never below - 2.

ACTIVITY

Criterion 8 Activity: A GR-EIGHT Formula

Directions: *Randomly select three Stories from this book. In each Story, identify and count the total number of Descriptive Sentences. Use that number as the dividend, DESCRIBE in the Social Story Formula. Count the total number of Sentences that Coach and use as the divisor. Divide DESCRIBE by COACH. Compare the results. The answers will vary, though they always will result in a number that is greater than or equal to two.*

FINAL NOTES

If a Social Story™ had a heartbeat, the Social Story™ Formula would be it. The Formula contributes to the patience and unassuming quality that distinguishes Social Stories™ from other visual strategies. It is a Gr-eight Formula that reminds Authors to take time to share information that people often assume that "everyone knows". It is the math behind an important Social Story™ standard: Every Social Story™ "describes more than directs."

The New Social Story™ Book, 15th Anniversary Edition
© by Carol Gray, Future Horizons, Inc.

The 9th Criterion: Nine Makes It Mine

DEFINITION

Every Social Story is reviewed and revised until it meets all applicable Social Story Criteria.

DISCUSSION

The discussion of this Criterion is incredibly short, in sharp contrast to its importance. The effort to ensure Social Story™ clarity, meaning, and interest begins with research and topic identification and continues throughout Story development and editing. Authors use the Audience Team as a resource as a story draft is distributed for review and feedback. This catches avoidable and regrettable mistakes early, while at the same time updating everyone on Story progress prior to implementation.

ACTIVITY

Criterion 9 Activity: Nine to Refine

Directions: *Select a story from your own experience or work, and check it against the criteria that we have discussed. Does it meet all applicable criteria? In other words, up to this point (excluding the final Criterion which guides implementation), is it a Social Story?*

The New Social Story™ Book, 15th Anniversary Edition
© by Carol Gray, Future Horizons, Inc.

FINAL NOTES

Criterion Nine sends a strong message to anyone who thinks developing a Social Story™ is a simple and easy task. Like almost anything that is genuinely worthwhile, learning to write a Social Story™ takes time, thought, and practice. Once the skill is learned, writing each Story takes time as well. Never to be regarded as a "quick fix" in the field, Social Stories™ are here for the long haul. Stopping to make sure that the story in hand is the "genuine article" is a part of what makes any story a Social Story™

The 10th Criterion: Ten Guides to Implementation

DEFINITION

The 10 guides to implementation ensure that the philosophy and Criteria that guide Story development are consistent with how it is introduced and reviewed with the Audience.

DESCRIPTION AND ACTIVITY

The Ten Guides to Editing and Implementation are each briefly described in this section. The focus of the 10th Criterion is different from the previous nine. The first nine criteria define the process that researches and identifies a topic, and the characteristics and editing of the final document. With the final Criterion, the focus turns to implementation. Like carrying the baton in the final leg of a marathon, the goal is the same as the all of the steps preceding it: to implement a Story with the same care and consideration given throughout its development.

In our discussion of the 10th Criterion, we will complete activities as we go. Select a Social Story™ and use it for all activities. It will help you create a plan to introduce and implement your Story.

1. Plan for Comprehension

Authors of Social Stories™ plan for comprehension. This is an opportunity to look one last time at the text and illustration, specifically with comprehension in mind. Could questions be added to go with the Story? Once the Audience is familiar with the Story, could blank lines replace omitted segments of text, to create a fill-in-the-blank check of comprehension? An Author creates a plan to build meaning into a Story and support comprehension. Ideas listed in the next section, Plan Story Support, often overlap.

2. Plan Story Support

Story Support includes resources and instructional techniques to support a Story as it is implemented. Is there anything that may support the Audience? What about placing the Story on PowerPoint®? Another idea: create a classroom poster that contains an important phrase from the Story. There are many possibilities. Each is dependent upon the specific Audience and topic. Activity: Consider your Story. How might you support Audience comprehension and participation as this Story is implemented?

3. Develop a Story Schedule

The review of a Social Story™ reflects the patience, positive attitude, and sound thinking that created it. A Social Story™ is always reviewed in a comfortable setting with a positive tone. If review of a story is forced, it is not a Social Story™. Never (never, never, never) force review, or use a story as a consequence for misbehavior. Common sense dictates review. Establish a predictable review schedule that is frequent enough to be effective, and infrequent enough to avoid needless repetition. Authors consider both the Audience and topic factors to develop a workable plan. Keep in mind that the Audience may not always need—or want—the Author or another adult to present or review a Story. Activity: Develop a tentative plan for Story review. Considering your Audience and the Story topic, decide how frequently the Story will be read.

4. Plan a Positive Introduction

A Social Story™ is introduced with the same matter-of-fact and unassuming quality of its text. For example, an Author may begin with a quiet and confident statement, "This is a Story that I wrote for you ..." With younger audiences, it often works well to sit at the child's side and slightly back, with your joint attention on the story. The key is to be calm and comfortable. Activity: Present your Story to your Audience.

5. Monitor!

Once a Story is in place, Team members monitor its impact. It's important to look for Audience responses that may indicate an interpretation of the text or illustrations that is different from what the Author intended. Authors are always highly curious about success. If all is going well, why? What the important elements that are contributing to this Story's effectiveness? Can those same elements

The New Social Story™ Book, 15th Anniversary Edition
© by Carol Gray, Future Horizons, Inc.

be a part of future Stories? In this way future Stories are tailored in response to what is learned from their predecessors.

6. Organize the Stories

One Story does lead to another. It's important to keep them organized! A three-ring notebook with a clear plastic cover works great. Simply insert a drawing or picture to create the cover. Computers are great file drawers as well, with file folders that make Stories easy to retrieve. Activity: Organization is easier when it is present from the beginning. Find a notebook, or create a computer file, and put your Story in it!

7. Mix and Match Stories to Build Concepts

There are many possible Stories and they accumulate quickly! Topics often reappear, similar to past Stories but requiring a different "angle" or focus, or more developmentally advanced information. If you have several Stories about parties housed in different places, consider making copies and placing them in one "parties" notebook. Or when using a computer, occasionally search frequent topics and place similar Stories together in a new folder.

8. Story Reruns and Sequels

I've never heard of a "retired" Social Story™! Long after it has been set aside, a Story may be reintroduced, like a rerun on television. Your Audience may also benefit from Story Sequels, where information from a previous Story is updated. In this case, the Audience may appreciate the familiarity of elements of the original Story, while benefitting from the updated information the current Story contains. This also helps to tangibly demonstrate the important ties between past and present topics.

9. Recycle Instruction into Applause

Recycling is popular. Social Stories™ may be recycled, too! A Story that originally introduces new skills, for example, may later be recycled into a Story that applauds their mastery. This is especially easy when Stories are developed on a computer. Simply pull up the original Story and save it with a new, related title. Revise the original text into a Social Story™ that praises the Audience for his or her newly acquired skills. Proudly review it with the Audience.

10. Stay Current

Information is traveling faster than ever. Stay current on the latest updates and ever-accumulating Social Story™ information. Stop by CarolGraySocialStories.com frequently. It is the official home of genuine Social Stories™, with the most recent, accurate and reliable information available.

VERY FINAL NOTES

Social Stories™ have a relatively short but active history. Originally fueled by grassroots enthusiasm, and later studied and confirmed as an evidence-based practice, they have earned the respect of parents and professionals, as well as the trust of their Audience. You are their newest Author. I personally wish you all the best. I invite you to expand your skills by attending a Team Social Stories™ or Social Stories™ Satellite Schools and Services workshop or presentation. May the Stories that you write inform, guide, and inspire your Audience.

CHAPTER 1

Learning with Stories

I Wrote These Stories for You

A LETTER FROM CAROL GRAY

Dear _____,

My name is Carol Gray. Until I was twenty-two years old, my name was Carol Schuldt. Getting married changed my last name.

My mom's name was Viola Schuldt. She really liked to take photographs. She especially liked to take photos that tell a story. She would take five or six photos, and display them together. People would know "the story" behind the photos, even without words. Sometimes, just one photo tells a story, or reminds us of one.

This is a photo of me at three years of age. It was taken in 1955. In the photo, I am at my Aunt Jeannie's home. It's a birthday party for my sister, Marilyn. That's Marilyn, smiling at the cake. I am sitting on Aunt Jeannie's lap. That's me on the bottom right edge of the photo. I remember this party, especially the doll cake. Look at my face. I really loved that cake. I was a little sad that it wasn't mine. My mom is standing, holding my sister, Elaine. Looking at Elaine's face, I think that maybe Elaine felt like I did. I think she loved the cake, too, and felt a little sad that it wasn't hers, too.

This photo (below, left) was taken in 1958. I am six years old. I am with my Grandma and Grandpa Schuldt. It was their anniversary. They had a big, important party. Everyone wore their nice clothes. My dress was scratchy around my waist. After a while, the headband I wore hurt, too. At the moment that this photo was taken, I was tired of wearing my nice-looking-but-uncomfortable clothes.

When I look at these photos, it reminds me of one thing that I have learned about parties. Many people think that parties are fun. I like them, too. A person may have sad or confusing moments, though, even during an activity that is mostly fun. I think it's helpful to remember things like that, and to share it with other people. That way, those people won't be surprised if it happens to them.

This was my home on Dorais Street in Livonia, Michigan. I lived here from 1956 until 1968. I grew up here. It is where I wrote my first story when I was six. My bedroom was on the first floor, across from my parents' bedroom. I had a journal that I would write in each night before I went to bed. I would write letters to me, to read when I got older and became an adult, so that I wouldn't forget what it was like to be a child.

I am much older now. I'm still writing stories. I try to remember—always—what it is like to be a kid. I keep reading stories, too, and listening to the stories that people tell me. That's how I have learned much of what I know.

I wrote the stories in this book for you. They describe people and places, and other topics, too. I hope that you like these stories, and that you may learn from them.

I wish for you a wonderful life story,

Carol

The New Social Story™ Book, 15th Anniversary Edition
© by Carol Gray, Future Horizons, Inc.

Learning with Stories

People learn from stories. People often tell one another their experiences. As they listen, they learn.

Once, my mom was teaching me to tie my shoes. She told me a story about how her grandfather taught her to tie her shoes. I tried it, practiced it, and learned how to tie my shoes.

Another time, I was afraid to go down the slide on the school playground. I wanted to try it. I stood and watched other children climb the stairs of the slide, sit on the top, and slide down. I wondered if I could do that. My kindergarten teacher, Mr. Burns, came up and stood next to me. He told me a story. When he was a boy, he was afraid of going down the slide, too. "Did you try it?" I asked. He said he did. Mr. Burns said it really helped to look up as he climbed the stairs. I thought that might work for me. I went down the slide, and it was okay!

Last Tuesday it was raining. I didn't want to wear my raincoat. My sister, Madison, said it might be better to "just wear it." Then she told me a story. One day last year, it was raining. She didn't wear her raincoat to school. She got wet. Madison was cold, damp, and uncomfortable for the first hour of class. I decided to wear my raincoat to be dry and comfortable.

I am learning each day. People keep telling me their stories. I will try to keep listening, and learning. ■

The Stories in This Book

The stories in the book were written for me.

This book has stories about me and my feelings. It has stories about growing, and a place called Fort Able. There's also a story titled "Maybe I Could Do That!"

This book has stories about people and places. This book has stories about my family, home, and school. It has stories about adults and children.

This book has stories about mistakes. Everyone makes those. It also has stories about changes. Changes happen all the time.

This book has stories about what people think, and what they say and do. It has stories about sharing, playing games, and how to win and lose.

This book has a story about Thomas Edison, and three stories about chewing gum.

This book has stories about Planet Earth. That's my home planet. It also has stories about wildfires and air travel. There are even stories about the evening news, and why people watch it.

There are other things, too, such as what people mean when they use the word *thing*. That's in the glossary.

There are many stories in this book. One hundred fifty-eight Stories to be exact. They describe life here on Planet Earth. ◼

My Story Album

I have a Story Album with photos of my life story.

I may choose to have photos of me in my album.
I am the main character in my story.

I may choose to have photos of favorite people in my album. They are important in my story.

I may choose to have photos of my favorite places in my album. They are the settings of my story.

The New Social Story™ Book, 15th Anniversary Edition
© by Carol Gray, Future Horizons, Inc.

I may choose to have photos of my favorite toys and things. They are the tools of my story.

I may choose to have photos of fun times in my album. They make fun memories in my story.

I may add photos to my Story Album, too, as I grow.

I may look at My Story Album to look at me, favorite people and places, nice toys and things, and fun times. ■

CHAPTER 2

Social Stories for Young Children

Introduction

I was approached earlier this year by a team from Future Horizons, the publishing company that printed and distributed the first Social Story book in 1992, and all but one of them since then. It was time for the second revision of *The New Social Story Book*. Five years had passed since the first 2010 revision. During the conversation, it quickly became apparent that a new chapter with Stories for young children was a top priority for this 2015 volume. Therefore, here it is, along with this introduction to help you write for the youngest Social Story Audiences.

From my experience, one of the most important steps in developing a Story for a young child is gathering the necessary information prior to placing anything on paper. Since many young children with autism cannot answer our questions or describe their understanding of a situation, observation takes on heightened importance. Consultation with others on a child's team is also important. The goal is to discover *the* topic: the missing information or misunderstanding that may underlie a child's current problematic response. This focuses content early in the writing process, saving the Author time and frustration and improving Story quality.

Social Stories for young Audiences are very short, most often complete in three to twelve sentences. Authors need to get to the point to keep Story length within the attention span of the Audience. This can be frustrating, especially where there are important details that need to be included. In this case, a *Social Story Set*, a collection of very short Stories, has been developed. Each Story describes one idea or concept related to the overall topic. Social Story Sets are usually introduced one Story at a time. Breaks between each Story keep Story review comfortable, positive, and within a child's ability.

Repetition, rhythm, and rhyme are familiar elements in early childhood literature. They create a reassuring and predictable format and may make stories easier to recall and apply in practice. For these reasons, these elements are often part of Social Stories for young children.

One final reminder: Half of all Social Stories applaud what the Audience currently does well. In other words, fifty percent of all Social Stories written for any individual focus on what he or she is doing right, a positive trait, or a mastered skill. This builds self-esteem, and may prevent the overall rejection of Stories observed with some children. Every achievement, talent, kind gesture, and/or learned concept is a potential Social Story topic.

I wish you the best as you write for the toddler or preschooler in your care. ■

I Wear Pull-Ups

My name is Jonathan. I wear pull-ups to catch and hold my pee and poop.

A pull-up catches and holds the pee and poop that I don't need anymore. When it's dirty we throw it away.

I wear pull-ups to catch and hold my pee and poop. ▪

Someday I Will Wear Underwear

My name is Jonathan. I am learning about toilets.

First, children wear pull-ups. Then they wear underwear.

I wear pull-ups. Someday I will wear underwear. ■

The New Social Story™ Book, 15th Anniversary Edition
© by Carol Gray, Future Horizons, Inc.

Children Grow Kind Of Slow

Children grow. Sometimes, an adult will look at a child and say, "You're growing up so fast!" If children really grew really fast, their feet would be farther away every time they looked down!

Compared to many of the animals on Planet Earth, children grow kind of slow. Their bodies change little by little. Hamsters are adults at six months of age. Kittens become cats within one to three years. Puppies become dogs between two and three years of age. Most people become adults between eighteen and twenty-five years of age.

Children are busy people. So, they may not notice that they are growing. Then, one day their clothing or shoes are too small. When this happens, being bigger may seem a little surprising.

Getting bigger is a part of growing up. Compared to some animals, children grow rather slow. That's why children often don't notice getting bigger until their clothes are too small. ■

Why Do I Need New Clothes?

I'm a child, and I am growing taller and bigger. All children grow. Their clothes stay the same size. For this reason, children's clothing fits for a few months or so.

The time comes when clothing is too small. Shoes may fit tight and toes may feel crowded inside shoes. Or, pants are tight or short. Sometimes, shirts get hard to button.

It's time for new clothes.

I need new clothes because I get bigger, and my clothes stay the same size. ■

The New Social Story™ Book, 15th Anniversary Edition
© by Carol Gray, Future Horizons, Inc.

What is a Fixture?

A *fixture* is something attached to a building.

This fixture is a sink. It's attached to a house with a pipe.

This fixture is a toilet. It's attached to a house with a pipe, too.

There are many fixtures in my house. ■

The New Social Story™ Book, 15th Anniversary Edition
© by Carol Gray, Future Horizons, Inc.

What is a Toilet?

A toilet is a bathroom fixture. Each toilet has a bowl, seat, and lid.

This is a picture of a toilet.

The New Social Story™ Book, 15th Anniversary Edition
© by Carol Gray, Future Horizons, Inc.

This is another picture of a toilet.

The New Social Story™ Book, 15th Anniversary Edition
© by Carol Gray, Future Horizons, Inc.

This is a picture of a toilet in my house.

A toilet is a bathroom fixture with a bowl, seat, and lid. ■

Why Do People Have Toilets?

This is a picture of a toilet. As people grow, they learn to use toilets to catch and hold their pee and poop.

Every toilet catches and holds pee and poop that people don't need anymore.

People learn to use toilets to catch and hold their pee and poop. ▪

The New Social Story™ Book, 15th Anniversary Edition
© by Carol Gray, Future Horizons, Inc.

Toilets Flush to Throw Away Pee and Poop

People learn to use toilets to catch and hold their pee and poop. They don't need the pee and poop anymore, so they *flush* it away!

Flushing is how a toilet throws away pee and poop that is no longer needed. Then the toilet is clear again.

Flushing a toilet throws pee and (or) poop away. ■

Toilets, Pipes, and Waste Treatment Plants

These are pictures of toilets. Toilets are fixtures that are attached to a pipe.

Pee and poop move through the pipe to a factory called a *waste treatment plant*.

In my house, toilets connect to pipes that lead to the waste treatment plant. ■

Chairs

A chair is a piece of furniture.

Furniture makes a room ready to use. Tables, beds, dressers, chests, and things like that are furniture.

People sit on chairs to eat, rest, read, relax, or work. People use chairs indoors and outdoors.

A chair is a useful piece of furniture. ■

The New Social Story™ Book, 15th Anniversary Edition

A Toilet is Not a Chair

A toilet is not a chair, that's for sure.

A toilet is a fixture with a pipe that takes pee and poop to a waste treatment plant. It has a safe seat with a space for pee and poop to pass through.

A chair is a piece of furniture. It has a solid seat. People use chairs for many reasons, but never to pee or poop.

A toilet is definitely not a chair, anytime or anywhere! ■

It's Safe to Sit on a Toilet

It is safe for a child or adult to sit on a toilet.

That's good to know, because many people need to use toilets each day.

The toilet seat is small enough to sit safely, with a hole that is big enough for pee or poop to pass through.

A toilet seat is a safe place to sit, pee, and poop. ■

The New Social Story™ Book, 15th Anniversary Edition
© by Carol Gray, Future Horizons, Inc.

This is a Story About Dogs. Just Dogs.

This Story is about dogs. Just dogs.

This is a photo of a dog. Sometimes people say, "This is a dog," when they see a photo like this.

The New Social Story™ Book, 15th Anniversary Edition
© by Carol Gray, Future Horizons, Inc.

This is a dog.

The New Social Story™ Book, 15th Anniversary Edition
© by Carol Gray, Future Horizons, Inc.

This is a dog.

This is a dog.

These are dogs and a pig. A pig?
A pig does not belong in this story.

That's better, because this is a story about dogs.
Just dogs. ▩

My Parents Take Care of Me

My name is Christopher. Mom and Dad take care of me.

Mom and Dad help me clean my room.

Mom and Dad get me food to eat.

Mom and Dad help me take a bath.

Mom and Dad teach me how to do new things.

Mom and Dad take care of me to help me be healthy and smart! ■

I Am Learning to Tie My Shoes

I amlearning how to tie my shoes.

I learned how to button. I learned how to zip.

Someday, I will be able to tie my shoes. ■

We Take Care of Frank the Goldfish

We *take care* of Frank the goldfish.

Frank can't clean his fishbowl or get his food to eat.

So, we clean Frank's fishbowl when it's dirty and we feed Frank his food.

Taking care of Frank helps to keep him healthy. ■

I Am Going to Start Preschool

This is my story about preschool. I am going to start preschool in _____ days.

My adult and I will try to think about what I may see at preschool. We can write it here:

1. _____

2. _____

3. _____

My adult and I will think about what I might do at preschool. We can write it here:

1. _____

2. _____

3. _____

There are things to see and do at preschool. Some of them may be in this story! ■

The New Social Story™ Book, 15th Anniversary Edition
© by Carol Gray, Future Horizons, Inc.

Getting to Preschool

Many children go to preschool. There are many ways to get to preschool.

Sometimes children ride to preschool in a bus.

Sometimes children ride to preschool in a car.

The New Social Story™ Book, 15th Anniversary Edition
© by Carol Gray, Future Horizons, Inc.

Mom and Dad teach me how to do new things.

There are many ways that children get to preschool. ■

While I Am at Preschool

I go to preschool. My mom and dad are busy, too!

When I have "Hello Time," my mom is driving to her school.

The New Social Story™ Book, 15th Anniversary Edition
© by Carol Gray, Future Horizons, Inc.

When I am working, my dad is working, too.

The New Social Story™ Book, 15th Anniversary Edition
© by Carol Gray, Future Horizons, Inc.

When we are cleaning up, my dad is on his way home.

When children are in school, adults are busy in other places. ■

My Toys

My toys belong to me. They are mine.

Many of my toys were given to me.

Some of my toys have my name on them.

I may play with my toys or share them with someone.

I have toys that are mine. ■

Toys that Are Not Mine

There are toys that are not mine. This is okay.

Preschool toys are not mine. Children learn to share preschool toys.

My brother, Sam, has toys. Some of them were given to him or have his name on them. He may play with them or share them with someone.

Some toys are not my toys. This is okay. ■

Staying Close to Mom

We are going to the store. It's important to stay close to my mom.

This is a photo of me.

The New Social Story™ Book, 15th Anniversary Edition
© by Carol Gray, Future Horizons, Inc.

This is a photo of my mom.

This is a photo of me staying close to my mom. This is called "sticking together" at the store.

I will try to stay close to my mom at the store. This is very, very, very important. ■

The New Social Story™ Book, 15th Anniversary Edition
© by Carol Gray, Future Horizons, Inc.

Sticking Together by Staying Together

My family is going to a museum. A museum is a big place.

Sticking together in a big place is smart and safe.

Most of the time, sticking together means staying close to one another.

My family is going to a museum. We will try to stick together to be smart and safe. ■

Sticking Together by Working Together

Sticking together is working together.

The last time we went to a museum, my sister had to use the toilet. We made a plan so she could visit the restroom safely. That's sticking together by working together.

Sticking together is working together to stay safe. ■

CHAPTER 3

Self Care

Washing My Hands

Sometimes, my hands get dirty. My hands touch items with germs all day long. My hands touch doorknobs and pencils and many other things that have germs. I can't see or feel the germs on my hands. That's because germs are very, very tiny. Even though I can't see germs, soap and water sends them away.

This is a list of steps people follow when they wash their hands:

- Go to the sink.

- Turn the water on.

- Get hands wet.

- Put soap on hands.

- Rub hands together.

- Rinse hands with water.

- Turn the water off.

- Dry hands.

Washing my hands is a healthy habit. I will try to follow these steps to wash my hands. ■

The New Social Story™ Book, 15th Anniversary Edition
© by Carol Gray, Future Horizons, Inc.

Taking a Shower in Ten Steps

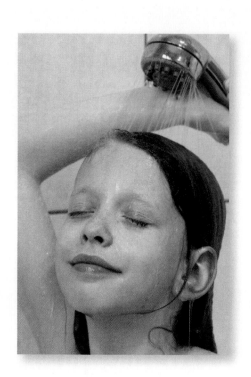

Many people use showers to get clean. Often, a person will say, "I'm going to take a shower." That means, *I am going to use the shower.* Soon, I will be learning to take a shower.

What follows is a list of steps that many people follow to take a shower at home. It is a list of what they do and why they do it.

TEN STEPS TO TAKE A SHOWER

- Go into the bathroom and close the door. Closing the door keeps a shower private.

- Take off clothes. This keeps clothes dry.

- Turn on the water and set a comfortable water temperature. If the water is too hot or too cold, a shower is uncomfortable. (Hint: Some people use the bathtub faucet to make sure the water temperature is comfortable, and then they send the water through the shower head.)

- Make sure the water is coming out through the shower head.

- Step carefully into the shower. Wet surfaces may be slippery.

The New Social Story™ Book, 15th Anniversary Edition
© by Carol Gray, Future Horizons, Inc.

- Wash hair with shampoo, rinse, apply conditioner, rinse. Shampoo is soap made just for washing hair. Conditioner makes hair easier to comb and style. Rinsing well after the shampoo and conditioner is important for clean and comfortable hair and scalp.

- Wash skin with soap. This gets a body clean. Rinse. Rinsing well is important for clean and comfortable skin.

- When the shower is done, turn off the water. This saves water and energy.

- Use a towel to dry skin and hang up the towel. Dry skin makes clean clothes feel more comfortable. Hanging up the towel keeps the bathroom neat. It also prevents someone from saying, "Hey, come back and hang up your towel."

- Put on clean clothes. Carry dirty clothes out of the bathroom. This helps to keep a bathroom neat.

I may use this list as I am learning to take a shower. My mom and dad know how to take a shower. If I have questions about taking a shower, they will know the answer. With practice, I may not need the list—or help from my mom and dad. I will have learned how to take a shower on my own! ▪

Sharing a Bathroom by Taking a Shorter Shower

In our home there are two bathrooms. One is for my mom and dad. The other is for me, my sister Emily, and my brother Austin, to share.

My sister Emily uses the toilet, shower, and sink in our bathroom.

My brother Austin uses the toilet, shower, and sink in our bathroom.

I use the toilet, shower, and sink in our bathroom.

Each of us needs to use the toilet, take a shower, and brush our teeth. To be fair, each of us needs time in the bathroom.

Shorter showers can help. When Emily takes a shorter shower, Austin or I can use the bathroom sooner. When Austin takes a shorter shower, Emily or I can use the bathroom sooner. When I take a shorter shower, Austin and Emily are able to use the bathroom sooner. Shorter showers help share a bathroom.

To share the bathroom with Emily and Austin, I will try to take a shorter shower. ■

How to Take a Shorter Shower

Sometimes it's important to take a shorter shower. Here's a list of ideas to make taking a shorter shower easier or more fun:

- Complete the steps to taking a shower, without playing in the bathroom.

- Set an alarm for ten minutes, and keep moving through the shower steps to finish before the alarm rings.

- Take a three-song shower. Record favorite songs on a shower radio. By the end of the first song, wash and rinse hair. By the end of the second song, wash and rinse skin. By the end of the third song, dry off and put on clean clothes.

At my house, it's often important to take a shorter shower. Having a plan can help. I may try using one of the ideas in this list. Or, my mom, dad, or I may have another idea. Whatever we decide, I will try to shorten my time in the shower to share the bathroom with others. ■

CHAPTER 4

Change

Change

People live on Planet Earth, and Planet Earth is always changing. As it does, people change, too.

There are many changes that people know will happen. Leaves fall to the ground. Water evaporates into air. Daylight darkens to night. People *expect* these changes.

Expected changes often form routines for people. Leaves fall to the ground; people rake them up. Water evaporates; people check if their plants need water. Daylight darkens to night; people go to bed. Expected changes form plans that become routines.

There are other changes that people try to *predict*. People know these changes may come, but they don't know for sure. So, they gather information. Then, they make their best guess. A sunny day changes with a thunderstorm. The night sky changes with a meteor shower. An earthquake breaks the surface of the earth. People try to predict when changes like these will happen.

The changes that people try to predict can *change* their plans. A thunderstorm causes people to have a picnic indoors instead of outside. A meteor shower causes people to watch the night sky instead of going to the movies. An earthquake causes a baseball game to be canceled. People try to predict the changes that can change their plans.

People live on Planet Earth, and Planet Earth is always changing. As it does, it helps people form routines, make plans, and causes people to change those plans, too. That's Life on Planet Earth. ◼

The New Social Story™ Book, 15th Anniversary Edition
© by Carol Gray, Future Horizons, Inc.

The Changes That Form Our Routine

Each day, there are changes all around me. A lot changes from day to night and night to day. Whether it is day or night helps people figure out what to do.

When the sun rises, the sky gets lighter. It's morning. For me, it's time for my morning routine. It's time to wake up, get out of bed, and start my day.

When the sun sets, the sky gets darker. It's evening. For me, it's time for my evening routine. It's time to put on my pajamas and get ready for bed.

Going from day to night or night to day is a big change. Going from night to day is a big change, too. The sun makes big changes that help me and everyone else know what to do! ■

A Theory about Change

Here is a theory: Expected and welcome changes are the easiest. Unexpected and unwelcome changes are the most difficult.

Life may seem simple by looking at a calendar. There's a box for each date. People often write their appointments and activities on a calendar. They finish the schedule for one day and then move on to the next.

For many people, changing from one day to another is easy. People go to bed expecting a new day, and welcome it the next morning. For many people, expected and welcome changes are the easiest for them to handle.

Unexpected changes are surprises. Some surprises are nice. For example, seeing a rainbow after it rains. Unexpected but *welcome* changes are often good surprises.

Some unexpected surprises are *unwelcome*. A flat tire on a car is an unexpected and unwelcome surprise. Unexpected and unwelcome surprises often mean that people have to do something they'd rather not do. Unexpected and unwelcome surprises are the most difficult changes for people to handle.

Life may seem simple by looking at a calendar. But each day isn't just the activities and appointments that are listed there. Some of life's most challenging events are those that are never written on a calendar. ■

My Theory about Change

Here's a theory: Expected and welcome changes are the easiest. Unexpected and unwelcome changes are the most difficult.

For many people, changing from one day to another is easy. It's an expected and welcomed change. One change that I like and expect is:

_____

For me, this change is (circle one):　　　EASY　　　CHALLENGING　　　DIFFICULT

Unexpected changes are a surprise. Some surprises are nice. For me, one unexpected but nice change (surprise) is:

_____

For me, this change is (circle one):　　　EASY　　　CHALLENGING　　　DIFFICULT

Some unexpected changes are also *unwelcome*. Unexpected and unwelcome changes often make people do something that they would rather not do. For me, an unexpected and unwelcome change is:

_____

For me, this change is (circle one):　　　EASY　　　CHALLENGING　　　DIFFICULT

Life may seem simple by looking at a calendar. But each day isn't just the activities and appointments that are listed there. Some of life's most challenging events are those that are never written on a calendar. ■

The Transformers around Us

BUTTERFLIES

Life is full of real transformers. They change their form—and how they look—following a biological plan.

A butterfly is a real transformer. Its life cycle is a biological plan with four stages. First, there's an egg that is laid on a leaf near butterfly food. It isn't an egg for long.

Second, the egg becomes a caterpillar. Caterpillars may have stripes or patches. They eat and grow. Their skin becomes too small. They shed it. A caterpillar grows fast. It may have to shed its skin four or more times.

The third stage is a pupa (also called a chrysalis or cocoon). This is the transformation stage. On the outside, a cocoon looks still. It's silent. On the inside, a lot is happening. The caterpillar is changing into a butterfly.

The fourth stage is the adult butterfly. Many butterflies have colorful wings. They can fly. They lay eggs, near food, that grow into caterpillars, and then cocoons, to become butterflies.

Some of the changes around us are transformations that follow a plan, over and over again. They are quiet transformations that are an important part of Life on Planet Earth. ■

The New Social Story™ Book, 15th Anniversary Edition
© by Carol Gray, Future Horizons, Inc.

The Transformers around Us

FROGS

Life is full of real transformers. They change their form—and how they look—following a biological plan.

A frog is a real transformer. Its life cycle is a biological plan with three stages. First, there's an egg that is laid in the water and covered with special jelly. It isn't an egg for long.

Second, the egg hatches. It's a tadpole! Sometimes, tadpoles are called polliwogs. Tadpoles eat and grow in the water. The top of the pond often looks still and silent. Under the water, a lot is happening. The tadpoles grow back legs, then front legs, and their tails shrink.

The third stage is a frog. People often think of frogs as green. A frog may be other colors, too. Some frogs change colors. Frogs lay eggs that grow into tadpoles, to become frogs.

Some of the changes around us are transformations that follow a plan, over and over again. They are quiet transformations that are an important part of Life on Planet Earth. ■

The Transformers around Us

LADYBUGS

Life is full of real transformers. They change their form—and how they look—following a biological plan.

A ladybug is a real transformer. Its life cycle is a biological plan with four stages. First, there's an egg. Ladybugs lay their eggs on the underside of leaves near ladybug food. They aren't eggs for long.

Second, the egg hatches. Larvae come out. Larvae look like insects, with six legs and tiny hairs on the side. They eat and grow for about twenty-one days. Then they begin to change.

The third stage is a pupa. This is the transformation stage. On the outside, a pupa looks still. It's silent. On the inside, a lot is happening. The larva is changing into a ladybug.

The fourth stage is the adult ladybug. They are red with black dots. They lay eggs, near food, that grow into larvae, and then pupa, to become ladybugs.

Some of the changes around us are transformations that follow a plan, over and over again. They are quiet transformations that are an important part of Life on Planet Earth. ■

The New Social Story™ Book, 15th Anniversary Edition
© by Carol Gray, Future Horizons, Inc.

I Am a Transformer

Butterflies, ladybugs, frogs, and ME!

I'm a transformer, too!

I once was a baby, but not anymore.

My smaller me definitely GREW!

I'm littler today than I will be soon,

I grow larger bit by bit.

I'm transforming again to a bigger me.

When I get to 'adult' size, I'll quit! ■

CHAPTER 5

Mistakes

What Is a Mistake?

A mistake is an answer, idea, or act that is an error. When someone says or does something that is not right, it's a mistake.

There are many examples of mistakes. It's a mistake to misspell a word. It's a mistake to leave a jacket at home on a very cold day. It's a mistake to forget to turn in finished schoolwork. People make many other kinds of mistakes, too.

As people grow, they learn from their mistakes. They may not make the same mistake again. However, people are always growing, and having new experiences. For this reason, people are always making new mistakes.

Sometimes, people know they have made a mistake. Other times, they learn that they made a mistake from others. Once in a while, a mistake is made and no one notices it.

Most people try to answer questions correctly. They try to have good ideas. They try to do the right thing. As hard as people may try, though, they still make mistakes.

Mistakes are a part of Life on Planet Earth. This is okay. ■

Thomas Edison and Mistakes

Thomas Edison was an inventor. Inventors have new ideas and create things for the very first time. Inventors make mistakes and know how to learn from them.

Thomas Edison made many mistakes. He stayed calm. That way, he could do his best thinking and learn from his mistakes. He helped to invent the light bulb and many other things, too. Thomas Edison expected to make mistakes. For inventors, mistakes are an important part of their work.

It's smart to know how to handle mistakes. Staying calm is important. A calm body helps a brain think and solve problems efficiently and effectively. (In this case, *efficiently and effectively* means that the brain is working at its very best!)

Many students learn to stay calm when they make a mistake. This helps them think well, and solve their problems efficiently and effectively. They learn to use mistakes to their advantage, just like Thomas Edison.

A brain works best in a calm body. Like many other students, I am learning to stay calm when I make a mistake. This will help my brain to work at its best! ◼

The New Social Story™ Book, 15th Anniversary Edition
© by Carol Gray, Future Horizons, Inc.

The Mistakes Survey

A *survey* is one way to get information about something. In many surveys, people are asked the same question or questions. Then, their answers are studied. I have a survey about mistakes.

Has anyone ever had a day without any mistakes? A survey is one way to learn what people think about this question.

My survey is titled *The Mistakes Survey*. I may use the survey to learn more about mistakes. My teacher knows how to use a survey. He may be able to help me.

The Mistakes Survey is for adults. To use the survey safely, it's important to give the survey to safe adults that I know, people who are not strangers. My teacher can help me to make a list of people to take this survey.

To take the survey, each adult will read this (it's at the top of the survey):

A *mistake* is an error. There are big mistakes, and little ones, too. Some examples of mistakes are:

- Doing something wrong, like making a wrong turn while driving or putting something together wrong

- Forgetting something, like being unable to remember someone's name or today's date

- Losing something, like important notes, keys, a shoe, etc.

- Dropping an item

- Making a calculation or writing error, including "typos"

There are many, many mistakes that people make.

Then they answer this question:

- Do you think that you have ever had a day without a mistake?

I will try to have five safe adults (from the list I make with my teacher) take The Mistakes Survey. After that, my teacher and I can talk about the answers on the survey. Together, my teacher and I may learn more about people and the mistakes that they make! ■

The Mistakes Survey

This is a survey about mistakes. Please read below and follow the directions.

A mistake is an error. There are big mistakes, and little ones, too. Some examples of mistakes are:

* Doing something wrong, like making a wrong turn while driving or putting something together wrong

* Forgetting something, like being unable to remember someone's name or today's date

* Losing something, like important notes, keys, a shoe, etc.

* Dropping an item

* Making a calculation or writing error, including "typos"

There are many, many mistakes that people make.

The New Social Story™ Book, 15th Anniversary Edition
© by Carol Gray, Future Horizons, Inc.

Please write your name, and circle YES or NO to answer the question.
Write comments if you wish.

Do you think that you have ever had a day without a mistake?

Name		*Circle One*

1. _____   YES   NO

Comment: _____

2. _____   YES   NO

Comment: _____

3. _____   YES   NO

Comment: _____

4. _____   YES   NO

Comment: _____

5. _____   YES   NO

Comment: _____

The New Social Story™ Book, 15th Anniversary Edition
© by Carol Gray, Future Horizons, Inc.

Mistakes Can Happen on a Good Day

I am learning that mistakes can happen on a good day.

Each day, many people make mistakes as they work and play. For example, they may forget their lunch, accidentally trip while going up steps, or dial a phone number incorrectly. There are more than a million other mistakes that people can make, too!

As people grow, they learn about mistakes. They learn that making a mistake is okay. A mistake is a mistake, and it's still a good day.

Most mistakes can be fixed. When I make a mistake, adults like my mom, dad, or teacher may be very helpful. They were children once and made a lot of mistakes. They may have made a mistake like the one I am trying to fix!

There's a lot of time in a day—24 hours, or 1,440 minutes, or 86,400 seconds to be exact. Usually, mistakes happen quickly. That leaves plenty of time to fix mistakes, and for other parts of the day to go well.

I am learning that mistakes can happen on a good day. ■

Can Mistakes Happen on a Good Day?

Can mistakes happen on a good day?
I guess it's possibly true.
With so many mistakes that people can make,
It's likely we'll each make a few.

So, do mistakes happen *every* day?
If people wake up, then yes.
But what if they all were to stay in their beds?
Well, *that's* a mistake, I guess.

Can mistakes happen on a good day?
It seems that maybe they do.
People make mistakes and *still* they say,
"Yes, I had a good day, and you?" ■

The New Social Story™ Book, 15th Anniversary Edition
© by Carol Gray, Future Horizons, Inc.

CHAPTER 6

Feelings

The People on Trevor's Team

Trevor is eight years old. These are photos of Trevor's Team. Every person on Trevor's Team loves and cares for Trevor. They want Trevor to be safe, comfortable, and happy. They teach Trevor, and want to help him grow to be a healthy and happy adult.

There are photos of My Team, too. Every person on My Team loves and cares for me. They want me to be safe, comfortable, and happy. They teach me, and want me grow into a healthy and happy adult.

My mom and dad can help me find Team photos to put in My Story Album. ■

What Is Comfortable?

Comfortable is a nice, safe feeling.

Comfortable may mean that nothing *on* my body hurts, scratches, itches, or stings. I don't feel cold or hot, I feel just right. My skin feels good. The skin on my head, nose, fingers, and toes feels good.

Comfortable may mean that nothing *in* my body hurts or aches. No head-ache or stomachache. No sprains or broken bones. No bad sounds. Nothing that tastes bad. I feel good inside.

Comfortable may mean that my *feelings* all feel good. I am not worried. I am not afraid. I do not feel sad, bad, anxious, or confused. For many people, knowing what to do, and how to do it, is comfortable. I feel happy, calm, and *comfortable*. My feelings feel good.

Comfortable may mean that a place or thing feels good and safe. There are things and places that feel nice and safe, like a chair or a favorite room.

Comfortable may mean that it feels nice and safe to be around another person.

Sometimes, everything in me and around me feels good. When that happens, I am *completely comfortable*. Comfortable is a nice, safe feeling. ▪

The New Social Story™ Book, 15th Anniversary Edition
© by Carol Gray, Future Horizons, Inc.

What Is Comfortable for Me?

Comfortable is a nice, safe feeling. What is comfortable for me?

Comfortable may mean that my skin feels good. I have clothes that are comfortable. Pajamas are often comfortable. Three types of clothing that are comfortable for me are:

_____

_____

_____

Comfortable may mean that I feel good inside. There are *comfort foods*. Comfort foods taste good and make people feel happy. Three of my comfort foods are:

_____

_____

_____

Comfortable may mean that my *feelings* feel good. There are things that I like to do. I often feel happy when doing those things. Three things that I like to do are:

_____

_____

_____

Comfortable may mean that a place or thing feels good and safe. There are things and places that feel nice and safe, like a chair or a comfortable room. Three places or things that are comfortable for me are:

_____

_____

_____

Comfortable may mean that it feels nice and safe to be around another person. Three people that are comfortable for me are:

_____

_____

_____

Sometimes, everything in me and around me feels good. When that happens, I am *completely comfortable.* Comfortable is a nice, safe feeling. ■

The New Social Story™ Book, 15th Anniversary Edition
© by Carol Gray, Future Horizons, Inc.

Happy Is a Comfortable Feeling

There are things that make me feel *happy*. Happy is a comfortable feeling.

I often feel happy when I play with my favorite toys. Some toys that I like to play with are:

_____

_____

I often feel happy about my favorite topics. A *topic* is a subject to think, talk, draw, or write about. Some topics that I like to think, talk, draw, or write about are:

_____

_____

Some people are very important to me. They try to keep me comfortable and happy. The people who are important to me are:

_____

_____

_____

Many people like feeling happy and comfortable. ▪

Looking for Smiles

Sometimes people smile when they are happy. If I were to look for smiles, where would I find them?

I may find them on children playing.

I may find them on moms reading stories to children.

I may find them on dads coming home from work.

Happy can happen almost anywhere, and a smile is often found there. ■

The New Social Story™ Book, 15th Anniversary Edition
© by Carol Gray, Future Horizons, Inc.

Smile! Why?

Most people like smiles. When people smile, the corners of their mouth go up and their teeth show. If their teeth don't show, that kind of smile is called a grin. Most of the time, when someone smiles, it means something nice.

A smile may mean, *I'm happy to see you*.

A smile may mean, *I'm having fun*.

A smile may mean, *I'm happy*.

A smile may mean, *I'd like to talk with you* or *I'd like to play with you*.

A small, gentle smile may mean, *I wish you felt happier*.

A smile may have other meanings, too.

Most of the time, when someone smiles, it means something nice. ■

What Is Uncomfortable?

Uncomfortable is a bad, sometimes-unsafe feeling.

Uncomfortable may mean that somewhere on my body hurts, scratches, itches, or stings. Bee stings, poison ivy, cuts, or scrapes can make skin feel uncomfortable.

Uncomfortable may mean that somewhere *in* my body it hurts or aches. A headache, stomachache, flu, a cold, sprained ankle, broken bone, or food that tastes bad can be uncomfortable.

Uncomfortable may mean that I feel worried, afraid, angry, sad, or bad. Feeling confused is uncomfortable, too.

Uncomfortable may mean that a place or thing is not comfortable to be near or around. Some people feel uncomfortable in a very small place. Other people feel uncomfortable on roller coasters. For many people, very loud, busy, or crowded places may be uncomfortable.

Uncomfortable may mean that it feels unsafe to be around another person. It often feels uncomfortable to be around a person who is angry or out of control. Sometimes, it may feel uncomfortable to be around a person who is doing something that most people don't do in that place, or in that way.

Uncomfortable is a bad and sometimes-unsafe feeling. ■

What Is Uncomfortable for Me?

Uncomfortable is a bad, sometimes-unsafe feeling.

Uncomfortable may mean that somewhere *on* my body hurts, itches, or stings. Scratchy clothes may be uncomfortable. Three other things that can make my clothes uncomfortable are:

_____

_____

_____

Uncomfortable may mean that somewhere *in* my body hurts or aches. A headache is uncomfortable. Three things that can make my body feel uncomfortable inside are:

_____

_____

_____

Uncomfortable may mean that I feel worried, anxious, afraid, angry, sad, or bad. Crying is uncomfortable. Three feelings that are uncomfortable for me are:

_____

_____

_____

Uncomfortable may mean that a place or thing is not comfortable to be near or around. Very hot weather is uncomfortable. A very cold bath is uncomfortable. Three places that can be uncomfortable for me are:

_____

_____

_____

Uncomfortable may mean that it feels unsafe to be around another person. It often feels uncomfortable to be around a person who is angry or out of control. Sometimes, it may feel uncomfortable to be around a person who is doing something that most people don't do in that place, or in that way. A time when I felt uncomfortable around a person was:

_____

_____

_____

Uncomfortable is a bad and sometimes-unsafe feeling. ■

The New Social Story™ Book, 15th Anniversary Edition
© by Carol Gray, Future Horizons, Inc.

It's Okay to Feel Sad, but Feeling Happy Is Better

Sad is an unhappy and uncomfortable feeling. It's okay to feel sad. All people feel sad sometimes. People may cry when they feel sad. When a person feels sad, it's important to find a way to feel better.

Brooke had an ice cream cone. Some of her ice cream fell in the dirt. She felt sad, and cried.

Connor had a problem. He left his stuffed monkey, Elroy, at his friend Luke's house. He felt sad.

Aaron's cat, Orson, ran away. Aaron and his family love Orson. They all felt sad.

When people feel sad, they try to look for a way to feel better.

Sometimes, people feel better when they see that *all* isn't lost. Brooke still had the cone in her hand, and there was some ice cream in there, too. She ate that and began to feel happier.

Sometimes, telling someone else about a problem helps. Connor told his mom that his stuffed monkey Elroy was at his friend Luke's house. Connor's mom helped Connor get Elroy. Connor was so happy to see Elroy again!

Sometimes, working with others can help. Aaron's family looked for Orson right away. They found him under the back porch. They were all very happy to find Orson!

Sad is an uncomfortable feeling. It's okay for people to feel sad. When people feel sad they try to find a way to be happy again. That's Life on Planet Earth. ■

Everyone Has a Fort Able

There's a place called Fort Able. Fort Able is a very strong and safe place. It is a place in each brain that's calm and comfortable. Many people use Fort Able to stay in control and do their best.

Each person builds their own Fort Able as they grow. Each person is unique; each Fort Able is, too. There's a lot that is up to the builder of each Fort Able, although others can certainly help. In front of every Fort Able, there are three steps that lead to the door. That's how the builder gets in.

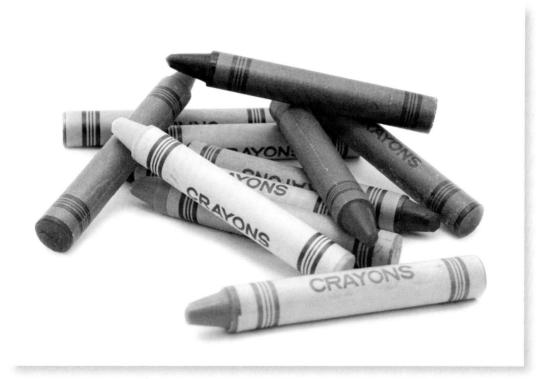

- In every Fort Able, there's a photo gallery. Photos of favorite people and fun times hang there.

- In every Fort Able, there's a media room. Favorite songs, movies, electronic games, and videos of fun times are stored there.

- In every Fort Able, there's a scrapbooking room. It's a room with anything and everything with a comfortable meaning or memory.

- In every Fort Able, there's a gymnasium. Healthy thoughts get exercise there. My Team and I will try to make a list of healthy thoughts for that room.

Every Fort Able comes with people who love the builder. They stand guard, and try to be ready to help in hard times, and cheer in good ones.

I have a brain, and a Fort Able, too. I'll try to draw you a tour, and be your guide through. ■

The New Social Story™ Book, 15th Anniversary Edition
© by Carol Gray, Future Horizons, Inc.

WELCOME TO FORT ABLE—SAMPLE (optional)

Welcome to Fort Able!

Welcome to Fort Able, the strong and safe place in my brain. This is the first stop on the tour. I'm the builder and owner of the place. I'm able to do my best thinking here. I'd like it if you could see it as I do, but it's not possible to squeeze you in through my ears, mouth, or nose. So, I will try to draw it for you, with three steps in front leading to the door.

Many forts are built with strong materials like wood, blocks, or cement. In the brain, people build with ideas and imagination. This is Fort Able from the outside. Of course, the goal is to stay *inside* the Fort.

THE PHOTO GALLERY—SAMPLE (optional)

The Photo Gallery

This is the Photo Gallery. Photos of favorite people and fun times hang here.

The New Social Story™ Book, 15th Anniversary Edition
© by Carol Gray, Future Horizons, Inc.

THE MEDIA ROOM—SAMPLE (optional)

The Media Room

In my Fort Able, this is the Media Room. Favorite songs, movies, electronic games, and videos of fun times are stored here.

THE SCRAPBOOKING ROOM—SAMPLE (optional)

The Scrapbooking Room

This is the Scrapbooking Room. It's a room with anything and everything that has a comfortable meaning or memory.

THE GYMNASIUM—SAMPLE (optional)

I am really good at soccer.

My parents love me a lot.

My teacher says I am a good student.

The Gymnasium

This is the gymnasium. Healthy thoughts get exercise here.

THE PEOPLE ON MY TEAM—SAMPLE (optional)

The People On My Team

These are the people on My Team. They stand guard, and try to be ready to help me in hard times, and cheer me on in good ones. I hope you enjoyed the tour. ■

Come to Fort Able

There's a place called Fort Able. Fort Able is a very strong and safe place. It is a place in each brain where a person finds calm and good control. It's easiest for a person to make smart and friendly choices there.

This is Luke. He looks comfortable, calm, and in good control. He's in Fort Able. When Luke is in Fort Able, he's able to make smart or friendly choices.

Sometimes Luke may feel uncomfortable. Sometimes he may feel very anxious, angry, sad, or confused. He's outside of Fort Able. That's an *un*-comfortable place to be! It's harder for Luke to think smart or be friendly. Where did Fort Able go?

Fort Able is always there. Luke has been in Fort Able many times before, and he will be there many more times to come. So, it must be there now, somewhere.

Whenever Luke feels uncomfortable, he takes the first step back to Fort Able. He says to himself, *Come to Fort Able, Luke!* Wherever Luke is, there's a way to Fort Able. Taking the first step is more proof that his Fort is nearby.

My name is _____. Fort Able is a place in my brain. It is where I make smart and friendly choices. If I feel I am out of Fort Able, I will try to find it again. There are three steps that open door. The first step is to say to myself, _____, *Come to Fort Able!* Or *ComFortAble* for short. ■

The Steps to Fort Able

There's a place called Fort Able. Fort Able is a very strong and safe place. It is a place in each brain where a person finds calm and control. It's easiest for a person to do their best there.

My name is _____. Fort Able is a place in my brain. It is where I am smart and make friendly choices. If I feel uncomfortable, out of Fort Able, I will try to find it again. The first step is to **SAY** to myself, _____, *Come to Fort Able!* Or, _____, *ComFortAble* for short. If I can't find the first step, I will try to get help from My Team.

The second step is to try to **THINK** of one of the rooms inside. Sometimes, just thinking about that room may help me feel better. I may be able to think smarter than I could a few mo-ments before. If I can't seem to find the second step, I will try to get help from My Team.

The third step is to **GO** inside. Once inside and comfortable again, I am able to do my best thinking. I may be able to solve the problem on my own. Or, My Team may be able to help me work things out, too.

There are three steps to getting inside:

- **SAY**—to myself, *Come to Fort Able!*

- **THINK**—of a room there.

- **GO**—inside.

I have a place called Fort Able. I built it myself. It's a strong and safe place, with three steps to the door, ***SAY-THINK-GO***. ▪

CHAPTER 7

Celebrations and Gifts

An Invitation to a Birthday Party

I have an invitation to Angela's birthday party. She is going to be six years old.

To guess what we will eat and do at Angela's party, I may try thinking of other birthday parties. Last year, I went to Tracey's party. There was a cake. We played games.

There is often a birthday cake at a birthday party. At Angela's party, there may be a _____.
There are often games at a birthday party. At Angela's party, there may be _____.

Angela is having a birthday. I'm invited to her party! ■

We're Going to a Big Family Party

Our whole, big family is having a holiday party. Last year we had a holiday party. There may be clues to what we will eat and do this year's party. My family is looking and listening for those clues, and making guesses about this year's party.

I will be going to the party with my mom, dad, my brother, Hunter, and our dog, Jasper. We're going to my Aunt Rhonda's house. Grandpa and Grandma Hill, Aunt Rhonda's boy-friend, Kevin, my Uncle Jess and his family, and my Aunt Rose and her family are invited to the party. *Invited* means they are welcome to come. Sometimes things happen, though, and people cannot come. We'll see for sure who is coming once we get to the party.

We had a big, holiday party last year. My dad has photos of last year's party in his computer. Dad says I may look at those whenever I want. Those photos help my family guess what we may do at this year's party. Some things may be the same. Some things may be different. Even if a party happens every year, it's never exactly the same as it was the year before. That would be impossible.

Last year, there was a lot of food. Some of it was adult food. I told my Grandma that the adult food looked pretty, but I did not want to eat it. There was good kid food, too. There were also a lot of desserts. Mom's guess is that there will be good kid food and desserts at this year's party. Last year, the people brought wrapped gifts. Hunter and I are hoping they will do that again! I told Grandpa Hill that I wish they wouldn't wrap the gifts. He says many people like to wrap gifts, so his guess is that they will wrap them this year, too.

Last year, I couldn't read. It was my job to give people gifts to open. Even though I couldn't read, it was easy. There was a small photo pasted to the corner of each gift. I would look at the photo, and take the gift to that person. I felt smart and important.

The New Social Story™ Book, 15th Anniversary Edition
© by Carol Gray, Future Horizons, Inc.

This year, my younger brother, Hunter, gets to give people gifts to open. Last year it was my turn. This year, it's Hunter's turn. I can read now. My mom says that even though I can read the to-and-from cards, it's important to stay quiet. It's important to let Hunter look at the photos and feel smart and important, like I felt last year.

My mom has been talking a lot on the phone to my Aunt Rhonda and Grandma Hill. They are making the plans for the party this year. Plans are clues to what may happen. Sometimes, plans can change, though. That's important to try to remember. Mom writes down the plans for this year's party. She lets me look at the plans whenever I want to.

My family is going to a big holiday party. The whole family is invited. My family is looking and listening for clues to what we will eat and do at this year's party. We find clues in photos. We find other clues in party plans. This year's party will give us photos and clues for *next* year! ■

What Is a Gift?

A gift is something special that one person gives to another person. A gift is often given to celebrate a birthday or holiday.

If I give a gift to my mom, my mom owns the gift. If I give a gift to my dad, my dad owns the gift. If I give a gift to a friend, my friend owns the gift.

A gift is something special that one person gives to another to keep. ■

The New Social Story™ Book, 15th Anniversary Edition
© by Carol Gray, Future Horizons, Inc.

Why Are Gifts Important?

Most people like gifts. They like to give them, and they like to receive them. Here are three reasons why gifts are important to people.

First, a gift helps people celebrate and share their feelings. A gift may mean, *I hope you have a happy birthday!* Or, it may mean, *I love you*, *Thank you*, or *Good luck*. It may mean something else, too, but it usually means something nice. That's why giving a gift can be so much fun.

Second, the person who receives the gift did not have to make it, or use their money to buy it. It's free. Many people think it's fun to get something for free, especially when it's something that is useful or nice.

Third, gifts help people remember friends, or family, and the fun times they have together. That's why many people keep the gifts that they receive for a long, time—sometimes even forever.

Gifts help people share and remember good times and nice feelings. ■

Why Do People Wrap Gifts?

Many people wrap gifts before they give them away. Why do they do this?

Wrapping hides a gift, and helps to keep it a secret. Later, when the gift is opened, it's a surprise. Many people think that nice surprises are fun.

A wrapped gift is pretty. Sometimes, there's colorful paper, a bow, or a card. Many people think that wrapping a gift is a beautiful way to hide a surprise.

Wrapped gifts are a part of celebrating special times and feelings.

Wrapping a gift hides a surprise. ■

The New Social Story™ Book, 15th Anniversary Edition
© by Carol Gray, Future Horizons, Inc.

How to Give Someone a Gift

It's important to learn how to give people gifts. Even though giving a gift is very nice, it may feel a little awkward the first few times. Knowing what to do helps to make gift giving easier.

When I give someone a gift, I only need to say a few words. For example, I may say, "Here's a gift for you," and maybe add to that, "I hope that you like it." If it's a birthday gift, I may say, "Happy Birthday." If it's a Christmas gift, I may say, "Merry Christmas!" If it's a gift for Hanukah, I may say, "Happy Hanukah!"

Often people will say "thank you" before opening a gift. They don't even know what is inside, and they are saying "thank you" already! Why? People know it takes time to find and wrap a gift. What they mean is, *Thank you for thinking of me and taking the time to get and wrap a gift for me.*

Sometimes, people open a gift right away. Other times, they wait until a later time.

At first, giving someone a gift may feel a little awkward. Learning what to do and say can help. It also helps to know what the other person may say or do. With practice, giving someone a gift becomes easier and more comfortable. ∎

How to Open a Gift

Sometimes people give me gifts. I am learning what to think, say, and do when I get a gift.

It takes time and sometimes money to find and wrap a gift. For this reason, it's thoughtful to say "thank you" right when I get a gift (even before I open it). This means, *Thank you for thinking of me, and for getting this gift ready to give to me.*

It may be okay to open a gift right away. Or, it may be important to wait until later to open a gift.

After I open a gift, it's important to say "thank you."

I am learning what to think, say, and do when I get a gift. When I get a gift, I will try to practice! ■

Why Wait to Open My Gift?

A gift has a nice surprise inside. Waiting to open a gift may be a little frustrating, especially for children. How can adults be so calm? Why would they ask children to open a gift later, instead of right now?

It helps to know what adults are thinking. Adults have as much fun waiting to open gifts as they do opening them. They like the festive feeling of sitting and talking among pretty gifts.

Adults may think it's polite to wait a while before opening a gift. That's why, at many parties, people eat, talk, or play games before opening gifts.

Visiting with the people who bring gifts is sometimes more important than opening the gifts that they bring. So, visiting is first.

Usually, adults decide when to open gifts. It may be now, but often it is later. Sometimes, knowing what adults are thinking makes it easier to open gifts later. ■

Learning to Stay Calm around a Wrapped Gift

A wrapped gift is often exciting. There may be something fun inside! *Excited* is often a good feeling.

Sometimes, an excited person is asked to wait. When this happens, excitement may feel a little uncomfortable. Knowing what to think, do, and say may help.

It's important to remember that adults often decide when gifts are opened. Many times, children may want to open gifts right away. But right away may not be a good time to open a gift.

It's important to know what to do with a wrapped gift. Learning to wait until it is okay to open a gift helps me and everyone else. Finding something to do until it is time to unwrap a gift may make waiting easier.

When there's a wrapped gift around, knowing what to say may help. It's okay for children to ask, "Is it time to open the gift?" It's important, though, to only ask that question a few times. This is because some people begin to feel grumpy if they are asked the same question too often.

Adults often decide when gifts are opened. If I have questions about why I need to wait to open a gift, I may ask an adult. ■

Some Gifts Are Disappointing

Most of the time, a gift is a nice surprise. Once in a while, a gift may be disappointing. This can happen when people give gifts to one another.

Sometimes, disappointment is a surprising sadness. A person is happy and expecting something nice to happen. But it doesn't. That person is sad, and surprised to feel that way. When this happens, *disappointment* is sadness that arrives fast and without warning.

A gift may be disappointing when it is something that is not wanted. Here's an example. Charlie gives Angela a book about dinosaurs. But, Angela isn't interested in dinosaurs. She thinks dinosaurs are boring. For Angela, getting a book about dinosaurs is disappointing.

A gift may be disappointing when it is something that is not needed. Here's an example. Parker likes rocks, and has a big collection of books about rocks. Parker gets a gift from his grandfather. It's a book about rocks. But Parker already has the book in his collection. He's disappointed because he doesn't need two books that are the same.

A gift may also be disappointing if the person opening it is hoping to receive one thing, and gets something else. Angela is hoping to receive a Barbie® doll for her birthday. She opens a gift from her grandmother. There are socks inside. Angela may be disappointed to see socks, because she was hoping to see a Barbie® doll.

Almost everyone is disappointed by a gift now and then. For this reason, parents teach their children about disappointing gifts. In this way, children learn what to think, say, and do when a gift is disappointing. ■

The New Social Story™ Book, 15th Anniversary Edition
© by Carol Gray, Future Horizons, Inc.

What to Think, Do, and Say If a Gift Is Disappointing

Someday, I may open a disappointing gift. It may be my birthday. It may be during the holidays. Most people are disappointed by a gift now and then.

When a gift is disappointing, knowing what to think may help. A disappointing gift is still a gift. Someone gave it to me. That person is hoping that I will like it. This is important to remember.

When a gift is disappointing, knowing what to do may help. Disappointment is a feeling that is best kept under my control. That way, I can be careful with the feelings of others. I will try to take control of my disappointment, and keep the feelings of others safe.

When a gift is disappointing, knowing what to say may help. I will try to say "thank you." Thanking someone for a gift—even if the gift is disappointing—is polite.

Some gifts are disappointing. Learning what to think, do, and say can help me get control of disappointment. With practice, I may be able to open a disappointing gift and keep the feelings of others safe at the same time. ■

CHAPTER 8

People Skills
and
Friendship

How to Greet Someone

There are many ways to greet someone.

When I see someone I know, especially if I am seeing that person for the first time that day, it's friendly to say "hello." They may say "hello," too. They may stop to talk with me.

Sometimes people shake hands to say "hello." Usually it is adults who shake hands to say "hello." For example, an adult may try to shake my hand if he or she is meeting me for the first time. This will happen more and more as I get older.

Once in a while, I go to visit relatives or close friends. A short hug as I arrive means *hello*.

Sometimes, if I am just passing someone I know, I may smile, wave, or just nod my head. If I said hello to that person earlier in the day, smiling, waving, or nodding my head means, *Hello again*. This is a friendly thing to do.

There are many ways to greet someone. I may think of other ways that people greet one another! ■

Why Do People Shake Hands?

People shake hands for many reasons.

They shake hands when they meet someone for the first time, or to greet someone that they have not seen for a while. Sometimes people shake hands as they leave a party or gathering. When people agree on a plan or a contract together, they may shake hands to "seal the deal." In each case, a handshake is used as a friendly gesture.

People who study history believe that people began using handshakes several hundred years ago in England. During that time, adults sometimes carried weapons. Men would sometimes hide weapons up their left sleeve. Extending the left arm, and shaking the hand of another person, was a gesture to show that neither person was hiding a weapon. Later, when carrying a weapon was not common anymore, handshakes switched to the right hand.

People shake hands for many reasons. It's likely that handshaking, with such a long history, will probably be a gesture that people will use for many years to come. ■

How to Shake Hands

As children grow, they learn about shaking hands. This is important, because adults often shake hands when they meet someone, or to say "hello." For this reason, I am learning to shake hands with adults.

Adults shake hands more often than children. Once in a while, though, children are expected to shake hands. This gives children practice with shaking hands, so they know how to do it before they become adults.

To shake someone's hand, I may try practicing these five steps:

* Reach forward with my right arm, right hand open.

* Grasp the other person's hand.

* Keeping the grasp, move my hand up and down.

* Open my right hand.

* Return my arm to my side.

Not very often, but once in a while, one person reaches forward to shake hands and the other person keeps their arm at their side. This may feel a little awkward. If this happens, it's okay to lower my arm without shaking the other person's hand.

Knowing how to shake hands with other people is important. For me, shaking hands with another person is likely to become easier with practice. ■

Two-Person Hugs

Sometimes two people hug one another. It's a two-person hug when both people hug at the same time.

A two-person hug often means *hello* or *goodbye*.

Sometimes, people use two-person hugs to share their feelings. These hugs may mean, *I love you*, *We are both happy*, or *We are both sad*.

When two people hug each other at the same time, they often:

- Stand close, facing each other

- Wrap one or two arms around the other person

- Squeeze a little but not a lot

- End the hug when either person begins to relax their arms

Sometimes two people hug each other at the same time. A two-person hug is a way to share feelings. ■

One-Person Hugs

People use hugs to share their feelings. Sometimes, two people hug each other at the same time. This is a two-person hug. Other times, one person hugs another. This is a one-person hug. A one-person hug has many possible meanings.

In a one-person hug, one person hugs the other. One person wraps one or two arms around the other person.

Sometimes, a one-person hug means, *This is my friend*. Children often do this. One child places their arms around another child. If the other child doesn't want to be friends, these hugs may be a little confusing.

Sometimes, people may use a one-person hug to help another person feel better. Moms and dads use hugs this way when their children are really sad, hurt, uncomfortable, or frightened. Sometimes, it works. Other times, it doesn't.

A one-person hug may mean, *Way to go* or *I'm proud of you*. Moms and dads use these hugs with their children. Sometimes, a coach may use a one-person hug with a player. Proud hugs may begin or end with a pat on the back, or a "high five."

A one-person hug has many possible meanings. ■

When It Is My Turn to Listen

People talk with one another. They have conversations. As they grow, people learn that listening to others is important. Listening helps to keep a conversation fun and interesting for everyone. Listening also helps people make friends. I am learning what to do when it is my turn to listen in a conversation.

To have a conversation, people learn to take turns talking and listening. While one person talks, the other person listens. If both people talk at the same time, which does happen now and then, they can't hear what the other person said. Taking turns works much better.

Listening is hearing words and thinking about what they may mean. Sometimes people mean what they say, other times they mean something else. This can make listening difficult. In fact, for many people, talking is easier than listening. For this reason, many people have to work hard to become better listeners.

When it is my turn to listen, I will try to hear the words that people say. I will try to think about what their words mean. My mom, dad, and teachers are ready to help me, as I learn what to do when it is my turn to listen. ■

Thanking People for the Nice Things That They Say

Sometimes people say something helpful or kind. Saying "thank you" after someone says something nice means, *What you said to me is helpful* or *What you said to me is kind*. There are many times when saying "thank you" is a smart and friendly thing to do.

Sometimes people help me. Yesterday, I had a question about our math assignment. Sydney sits next to me in class. She remembered the assignment. She said, "We have to do all the problems on page 32." I said, "Thanks." That's a shorter way to say "thank you."

Sometimes people say kind things to me. Last week on my birthday I wore a new shirt to school. My teacher said, "Happy Birthday! Nice shirt, too!" It's easy for people to remember their own birthday, harder to remember someone else's birthday. I said, "Thanks," to my teacher.

Thank you is a friendly phrase that means, *It was nice of you to say that!*

I will try say "thank you" when people say nice things to me. That way, they will know that I heard the nice things that they said to me. ■

The New Social Story™ Book, 15th Anniversary Edition
© by Carol Gray, Future Horizons, Inc.

Thanking People for the Nice Things That They Do

Sometimes people do nice things for me. Saying "thank you" after someone does something nice means, *What you did for me is helpful* or *What you did for me is kind*. There are many times when saying "thank you" is a smart and friendly thing to do.

Sometimes people help me. Yesterday, Mary let me borrow her pencil. If someone helps me, I will try to say "thank you."

Sometimes people share with me. When I play at Aiden's house, we play with his toys. Aiden shares his toys with me. When someone shares with me, I will try to say "thank you."

Thank you is a friendly phrase that lets others know that I like the things that they do for me! ■

Learning to Help Others

Helping is doing something for another person. Being helpful is kind and thoughtful.

Sometimes people ask for help. My mom may ask me to carry a bag. She needs my help. Or, my dad may ask me a question about the computer. He needs help.

Other times, people may need help but do not ask for it. When this happens, it's very nice to offer to help.

There are many ways that I can be helpful. ▪

Helping People Who Haven't Asked for Help

Many people need help. They may not ask for help, but they sure could use it. It's very nice when others see that help is needed.

People often need help when it's difficult to complete a task alone. It's difficult for a mom with a stroller to open a door. Holding the door open is helpful.

People often need help when they are doing something for the first time. There's a new boy in my class, and it's time for lunch. He's never been to lunch at my school before. He may need a little help to learn about how we get lunch at our school.

People often need help when they are in a hurry. When people are in a hurry, they try to do things faster. Offering to do one of those things makes their job easier.

If I look for people who need help, I may find them just about anywhere, doing just about anything. That's because people often need help. ◼

It's Easiest to Help People Who Want Help

People often need help. They need help when a task is difficult to do alone. They may need help when doing something for the first time. Or, they may need help when they are in a hurry.

If I notice a person who needs help, I may offer to help. My sister just learned to tie her shoes. She is practicing, but it still takes her a while to make the bow. I have been tying shoes for many years. I can tie shoes quite fast. Once in a while I might offer to help my sister tie her shoes. I may start by saying, "Do you want help tying your shoes?"

It's important to listen carefully for her answer. This is because it is easiest to help people who want help.

When people want help, they cooperate with it. If my sister wants help with her shoes, she'll cooperate with me. She might hold her foot so that I can tie her shoe easily. Or, she may smile because that help is here. Cooperation is a clue that my sister is happy to have my help.

Most of the time, it's easiest to help the people who want my help. ■

It May Be Difficult to Help People Who Don't Want Help

People often need help. They need help when a task is difficult to do alone. They may need help when doing something for the first time. Or, they may need help when they are in a hurry.

If I notice a person who needs help, I may offer to help. Math is easy for me. Math is difficult for my brother. Once in a while I might offer to help my brother with his math homework. I may start by saying, "May I help you with your math?"

It's important to listen for his answer. This is because it is easiest to help people who want help.

My brother may not want my help. He may say, "No," shake his head to mean no, or turn away. All or any of these mean that my help is not wanted now. At another time, my brother may want help with his homework.

There are many reasons why someone may not want help. My brother may want to complete his math assignment by himself, to feel grown up. Or, he may want my mom or dad to help him.

When I offer to help and the answer is "no," this is okay. Unless the person is in real danger, it's okay to go and do something else. Sometimes, people feel a little sad when they offer to help and their help is refused. I may feel sad if my help is refused. Knowing that there are other people who want my help may make me feel better.

Sometimes people need help, but don't want help. When this happens, it may be a smart choice to do something else. There are many other people who need and want my help. ■

What Is Sharing?

I am learning about sharing. There are times when someone asks me to share. My mom may ask me to share. My dad may ask me to share. A classmate may ask me to share. Knowing what sharing is, and why people do it, may make it easier to share.

Sometimes, a share is a part of something. If someone has a great big chocolate cake, and there are twelve people who want chocolate cake, each person gets their share. Their piece of the cake is their share. And if each share is the same size, it's fair, too!

Other times, a share is a part of something—but each share is not the same thing or size. Sharing a lunch is like this. I may have a sandwich, an apple, and a bag of crackers in my lunch. If I decide to eat the sandwich and apple, and give the crackers to a classmate, that's sharing my lunch.

People can also share one thing that can't be broken apart. When four children sit on a sofa, they share the sofa.

People also share by taking turns. The people in my family share one computer. Each person uses the computer differently. Mom sometimes uses our computer to get recipes. My sister uses it for her homework. We can't all use it at the same time. So, each person has a turn using the computer.

As children grow, they learn to share. Many children discover that sharing is often a nice thing to do. Sharing helps make friends, too. My mom and dad were children once. As they grew, they learned how to share. They can answer my questions about sharing.

As I grow, I will try to learn more about sharing. ▪

What Is Respect?

I am learning about respect. *Respect* is being careful and thoughtful with other people. People show respect with kind words and actions. Respect helps everyone feel welcome, comfortable, and safe.

At home, parents and children show respect when they use kind words and actions. Respect helps a family to feel comfortable and safe.

At school, teachers and students show respect when they use kind words and actions. Respect helps everyone in a classroom feel comfortable and safe.

I will try to be careful and thoughtful with other people. I will try to use kind words and actions. I will try to use respect to help everyone feel welcome, comfortable, and safe. ■

The New Social Story™ Book, 15th Anniversary Edition
© by Carol Gray, Future Horizons, Inc.

Saying What I Think with Respect

I am learning about respect and feelings. All children have feelings. Adults often teach children to talk about their feelings. Learning to tell others how I feel is an important skill. Learning how to talk about feelings with respect is the next step.

Usually, when children are happy and comfortable, it is easier for them to talk with respect. This may be true for me, too. When I am happy, it may be easy for me to talk with my calm voice and cooperative words. At the same time, I am talking with respect, too.

Sometimes, children feel frustrated or angry. When this happens, it is more difficult for them to talk with respect. It's important to share these feelings. It's also important, though, to try to use a calm tone of voice and cooperative words. This takes practice.

I have My Team. My mom, dad, and teacher are on My Team. If I am angry or frustrated, My Team will help me to talk about my feelings with respect.

As I grow, there will be times when I feel angry or frustrated. Practicing with My Team will help me to feel anger—and show respect to others at the same time. ■

Restating with Respect

I am learning about respect. Many children make mistakes with respect sometimes. This is called being disrespectful. They may use a disrespectful tone of voice or words. This can hurt others' feelings or cause them to feel insulted or angry.

Learning to talk with respect is a skill. That's why children sometimes make mistakes with respect. Children need to think, and practice, to talk with respect.

When children make mistakes with respect, adults can help. When adults hear a disrespectful tone of voice or words, they will try to stay calm and say, "Restate with respect." This gives children a chance to think and try again, using a calm tone of voice and cooperative words.

When an adult says to me, "Restate with respect, please," I will try to think and say it again using a calm voice and cooperative words. This will help to keep everyone's feelings safe as we work and learn together. ▪

Using "Excuse Me" to Move through a Crowd

Once in a while, I will be one person in a crowd. A crowd is many people sharing a space together. Often a crowd of people have to stand close together to share the space that is available. This makes it difficult if one person has to get through the group to another place.

Here's an example. A popular movie opened last week at our movie theatre. My dad and I went to see it. We already had our tickets, and wanted to get some popcorn. There were many people waiting in the lobby for the theatre doors to open. The popcorn was on the other side of the lobby from my dad and me. This was a good time for me to practice what to say and do to move through a crowd.

I began by facing the line for popcorn. Then I said, "Excuse me." People began to move aside, so once in a while, I would say, "Thank you." I kept moving slowly. I had to keep repeating "excuse me" every few steps. That way, I could use a friendly voice that wasn't too loud for a movie theatre lobby. A little smile seemed to help, too.

With me in front and Dad behind me, we made it to the popcorn line a few slow steps at a time. Dad says he's proud that I practiced using "Excuse me" at the theatre. I felt proud, too, to see it work! ■

Learning to Chew Gum

I am learning about how people chew gum.

Sometimes gum comes in a wrapper. This keeps it clean. It's important to take the gum out of the wrapper before putting it in my mouth. Some people save the gum wrapper to use again when they are done chewing the gum.

When gum is done, it is thrown away. When I am done chewing my gum, I may cover it with the gum wrapper and put it in a waste basket.

Many people, like my mom, dad, and grandparents, know how to chew gum. If I have questions as I learn about chewing gum, they can help. ■

The New Social Story™ Book, 15th Anniversary Edition
© by Carol Gray, Future Horizons, Inc.

Three Gum Manners That Matter

Gum can be fun until it's done. Knowing about gum manners makes gum fun for me and those who choose not to chew.

There are three gum manners that matter. They are important because they keep gum from looking gross while it is being chewed. Also, Gum Manners keep gum where it belongs. That way, it doesn't make a mess.

First, gum is made for chewing. It's a good idea to keep the gum in my mouth until I am ready to throw it away. Sometimes, a person may chew gum, take it out, and chew it again, over and over. This is a mistake. It's not a healthy idea. I will try to leave my gum in my mouth until I am finished chewing it.

Second, chewing gum with the mouth closed helps others. Many people do not want to see gum being chewed. It's a little gross. That's why people who chew gum try to keep their mouths closed. When I chew gum, I will try to think of how it looks to others. I will try to keep my mouth closed.

The third gum manner matters long after the gum is chewed. It's about how gum is thrown away. Used gum belongs in a waste basket. It's sticky. If it is left anywhere else, it will stick to whatever comes along. Sometimes, that is somebody's shoe. Other times, it's somebody's clothing. To keep gum from sticking to other people, or to other things, it's important to throw it away correctly.

If everyone in the entire world followed the three gum manners that matter, no one would be grossed out by seeing gum being chewed or getting used gum stuck to them. I will try to remember and follow the three gum manners that matter. ■

The New Social Story™ Book, 15th Anniversary Edition
© by Carol Gray, Future Horizons, Inc.

What to Do When I'm Done with My Gum

When chewing gum is done, the best plan is to wrap it in a small piece of paper before throwing it away.

Sometimes, people save the gum wrapper in a pocket while they are chewing the gum. Then, when the gum is done, they use it to wrap the gum before throwing it away. This is a good plan.

If a person doesn't have a small piece of paper, its okay to throw gum into a waste basket without it.

When I am done with my gum, I will try to wrap it and throw it away in a waste basket. ■

Games Based on Luck

Sometimes, children play board or card games. Many children like to play games. I am learning about games, and how to stay calm and in control when I play them. Some games are based on luck.

If a game is based on luck, it means that there's nothing a player can do to win or lose the game. Players win because of luck.

Candy Land® is a game based on luck. Children or adults win Candy Land® because they select the cards that get them to the finish line first. They do not have to think of a correct answer, or decide what to do, to win. They win because they were lucky to select those cards.

Many children learn to stay calm if they win or lose a game based on luck. That way, others may want to play the games with them again!

Sometimes I may play a game based on luck. Sometimes I may win. Sometimes I may lose. Winning or losing is not up to me or how I play. It is up to luck. I will try to stay calm and in control when I play a game based on luck. ∎

The New Social Story™ Book, 15th Anniversary Edition
© by Carol Gray, Future Horizons, Inc.

Games Based on Skill

Many children like to play games. They play board or card games, or team sports. I am learning about games, and how to stay calm and in control when I play them. Some games are based on skill.

When a game is based on skill, players try their best to win. Chess is a game based on skill. The Olympic games are based on skill. Players win these games by using their skills. Luck may also help, but skill is most important.

Many times, very smart and skilled players lose skill games. They try to stay intelligent and calm. They try to learn from their mistakes so they may win the next time.

Team sports are based on skill and teamwork. Players work together for a goal, like making baskets in basketball or a home run in baseball.

Sometimes I may play a game based on skill. I will try to win, whether playing on my own or as part of a team. Sometimes I may lose. Win or lose, I will try to stay calm and in control. ■

How to Lose a Game and Win Friends

Children often play games. Sometimes I play games with others. I may win a game. Other times, another person wins. This happens when people play games.

Winning is often a good feeling that is easy to control. Losing is harder to handle. Knowing how to lose can help me keep friends.

Children like to feel safe and comfortable when they play games. When they play with someone who suddenly becomes very upset, it can be a little frightening. It's not much fun. It feels uncomfortable. For this reason, staying in good control of feelings is one way to make and keep friends.

As children grow, friends become very important. So, they learn what to think, say, and do to stay in control when they lose.

First, here are some thoughts that help children stay in control when they lose:

- "I want the other children to play with me again sometime."

- "Oh well, I did have fun playing the game."

- "I may win the next time."

A child may think of something else to stay in good control, too.

The New Social Story™ Book, 15th Anniversary Edition
© by Carol Gray, Future Horizons, Inc.

Second, when a child loses he may say,

- "You won!" or

- "Good game!" or

- "Good job!" or

- "Oh boy, and I thought I was going to win." or

- "Let's play again."

There are many other friendly things to say, too.

Third, a child learns what to do to lose a game and win friends. He may:

- Take a slow, deep breath

- Ask to play the game again

- Tell the winner that she played well, or

- Choose to do something else.

The important thing to do is to try to stay in control.

I will try to practice what to think, say, and do to lose a game and win friends. ■

After a Game Ends

Many people enjoy playing games. Most of the time, a game ends when someone wins. "I won!" also means that the game is over.

Games are fun, but it's good that they end, too. That way, people can go and do other things.

Once in a while, it's *very* good that someone wins. Everyone is getting a little bored. They are very happy when the game ends. Finally, they can go and do something else. Sometimes, everyone is *so* happy when someone wins and the game ends, it's like everyone won!

Other times, though, a game is really fun. Suddenly there's a winner. The game is over. This is okay. Someone may say, "Let's play again!"

Most of the time, when someone wins the game ends. People are free to go and do other things, or to play the game again. ■

CHAPTER 9

Bullying: What to Think, Say, and Do

Introduction to Bullying

WHAT TO THINK, SAY, AND DO

This is a very important chapter. Together, the Stories in this chapter describe how to *respond* to a child who bullies. They describe what to *think, say,* and *do* if someone tries to bully me. It is important to begin with some information.

Most students are *kind*. They *want* all students to feel *safe* and *comfortable* at school. *Almost* all of the time, kind students use friendly words. *Almost* all of the time, kind students *try* to follow the rules and help others. Sometimes, these students make *social mistakes* with one another. They may forget to share. Sometimes, kind students do not follow the rules. Soon, they want to make things right again. Adults help them learn from their social mistakes.

There are other students, not nearly as many in number, who attempt to bully others. They try to hurt another person's body, possessions, feelings, or friendships. These students are making a serious social mistake. They are out of control.

This chapter will help me to form a Team. My Team and I will learn about students who try to bully others. My Team will help me practice what to think, say, and do if someone tries to bully me. Together, we will learn and practice, working together to make each day at school safe and comfortable for me. ■

What Is Bullying?

Some students try to *bully* others by making them feel uncomfortable, frightened, or sad. They try to bully students who are *smaller or who have less power*. How can I know if someone is trying to bully me? It *may* be bullying if someone:

- Says something to me that is not kind, not true, or frightening

- Calls me by a name that is not mine, or that is unkind

- Writes messages that are not kind or that frighten me

- Hurts my body; for example, hits, trips, kicks, shoves, or pushes me

- Tells other students not to talk or play with me

- Asks me to do something that I know an adult would not ask, or want me to do

- Tells me to give them money, and not to tell an adult about it

- Makes the same or similar mistake many times, *over* and *over*

There are many other ways that a student may bully, too. No one can predict exactly when someone may try to bully another person. No one can predict exactly what a student may do in a bullying attempt. What we do know is that students who bully are out of control.

It's important to know what to think, say, and do if someone tries to bully me. That way, I will be ready whatever the student who bullies tries to do. ■

Which Students Try to Bully Others?

Bullying can be very confusing. Getting more information can help. A student who bullies may be a boy or a girl. A student who bullies may be older or younger than me. A student who bullies may be alone or with others. A student who bullies may:

- Do something that makes other students laugh

- Do something that causes an adult to feel upset or angry

- Do something that I know is wrong, or that I guess may be wrong

- Use an unkind face and words

- Use a friendly face and confusing words

If I feel confused or have questions about bullying, it's a smart decision to get more information from adults. Adults were children many years ago. They remember students who bullied them. An adult can help me decide if someone is trying to bully me. ■

The New Social Story™ Book, 15th Anniversary Edition
© by Carol Gray, Future Horizons, Inc.

My Team

I know some adults who are concerned about bullying. They are on *My Team*. My Team will work with me to make sure my school and neighborhood are safe and comfortable. I am an important member of the team. We work together. My Team will help me finish this chapter. Below is a picture of me with My Team. The members of My Team will print their names below their picture. They may *sign* their names, too.

Sometimes, a student may try to bully me when My Team is not around. Sometimes, a student may try to bully me when a member of My Team is near, but does not see the bullying. I can learn how to *respond* to a student who bullies. I can learn what to *think*, *say*, and *do*.

When a student tries to bully someone, it is called a *bullying attempt*. Reading Stories number 79-81 and completing all activities will help us to fill in the blanks on the following page about what to think, say, and do in response to a bullying attempt.

My Team is doing many things to make my school a comfortable and safe place for all students. They have been busy studying and learning new ways to respond to bullying. Even adults have to learn new skills. Later in this chapter, My Team will write a list of what they have learned. They will also write a list of what they are doing to keep our school and neighborhood safe and comfortable for all students. ▪

What to Think in Response to a Bullying Attempt

There are three steps to responding to a bullying attempt.

STEP 1: Calmly think about my bullying facts, and calmly think about a peaceful picture.

Calmly Think about Bullying Facts

Facts are true. Thinking about the bullying facts may help a student stay calm. If I am bullied, thinking about the bullying facts may help me use good self-control. There are many bullying facts. Here are three of them:

- It is not my fault that I am the target of this bullying attempt.

- The student who is attempting to bully me is out of control.

- I am not the only student who is bullied.

I have a choice. I may choose one, two, or all three facts to memorize and write it in the thought symbol on the next page.

Calmly Think about a Peaceful Picture

If I am bullied, thinking of a peaceful picture may help me stay calm and in good self-control. I may choose or draw a peaceful picture to put in my thought symbol.

A member of My Team will help me practice STEP 1 to responding to bullying attempt. STEP 1 is: *Calmly think about my bullying facts, and calmly think about a peaceful picture.* ■

What To Say in Response to a Bullying Attempt and How To Say It

There are three steps to responding to a bullying attempt.

STEP 1 is:

_____

STEP 2 is: Say one sentence well.

Knowing what to say and how to say it helps a student use good self-control.

What to Say

There are three sentences in the list below. I may choose one of these sentences. I will try to choose the one sentence that is the most true for me and the easiest for me to say. This is to be written in the talk symbol. This one sentence is what I will try to say in response to a bullying attempt.

- "I hear you."

- "I need you to stop."

- "I don't like that; stop it."

I have a choice. I may choose one sentence and write it in the talk symbol below.

When I say my one sentence, the student who bullies may keep talking. This can happen when a student is out of control. I have said my one sentence. I am finished. It's time to go. It is right to leave a bullying attempt, even if the student who bullies is still talking. This keeps me mistake-free and in good self-control.

How To Say It

I have facts and a picture to think about to help me stay calm. I have one sentence to say. As I say the sentence, I will try to:

- Keep all parts of my body to myself

- Stand straight with my head up

- Use a steady in-control voice

- Keep a safe distance

- Walk away after one sentence

Knowing what to say and how to say it takes practice. A member of My Team can help me practice. STEP 2 is: *Say one sentence well.* ■

What To Do in Response to a Bullying Attempt

There are three steps to responding to a bullying attempt.

STEP 1 is:

_____

STEP 2 is:

_____

STEP 3 is: Report the bullying attempt to a member of My Team.

Knowing why a report is important, what to report, how to report it, and whom to give my report to helps me stay in good self-control.

I may write "Report the bullying attempt to a member of My Team" in the arrow-shaped action symbol on the next page.

The New Social Story™ Book, 15th Anniversary Edition
© by Carol Gray, Future Horizons, Inc.

Why is it Important to Report Bullying Attempts?

Reporting is how people learn about important events that occur in other places. Often, an adult is not present when someone makes a bullying attempt. Sometimes, an adult may be present, but does not see the bullying attempt. My Team and I will make a plan for reporting bullying attempts. That plan will include deciding what to report, how I will make my report, and who will receive my report.

What to Report

Like news reporters, it is important for all students to learn how to carefully report bullying information to adults. A good report will include:

- Where the bullying attempt occurred

- When the bullying attempt occurred

- Who made the bullying attempt

- What was said and done during the bullying attempt.

How to Report

My Team and I will make a plan for reporting that is immediate, factual, and that works well for everyone on the team.

The best reports of bullying attempts occur right after the attempt happens. That way, it is easiest to remember the facts to describe the bullying attempt. This is very important.

The best reports of bullying attempts are factual. A factual report uses true sentences to describe where the bullying attempt occurred, when the bullying attempt occurred, who made the bullying attempt, and what was said and/or done. A student leaves a bullying attempt and tries to immediately make a factual report to a team member.

The New Social Story™ Book, 15th Anniversary Edition
© by Carol Gray, Future Horizons, Inc.

The first part of the plan is deciding how a student will report bullying attempts to the Team. Some students talk with a Team member to report a bullying attempt. Some students write to a Team member to report. Some students report bullying attempts by using a reporting form. Every Team has its own best plan. My Team and I will fill in #3 in the plan below. This completes the first part of our plan.

The second part of our plan is deciding who receives my report. Each adult member of My Team knows how to help when I have a report. Sometimes, one member of My Team may be sick or in another place. This is okay. There are other members of the Team. They are listed in order. I will try to give my report to the Team member at the top of the list. If that person is not nearby, then I will try to report to the Team member on the next line, and so on. It is important to report to a member of My Team. ■

My Team's Plan for Reporting Bullying Events

I will try to:

1. Report bullying attempts right away
2. Use facts to report bullying attempts.
3. Report bullying attempts by:

Adult Team Members will try to:

1. Listen to or read my report right away.
2. Clarify the facts if necessary.
3. Take helpful action.

_____

_____

I will give my report to:

1. _____. If not nearby, I will give my report to

2. _____. If not nearby, I will give my report to

3. _____.

What My Team Has Learned about Responding to a Bullying Attempt

A FACTUAL REPORT BY THE MEMBERS OF MY TEAM:

_____

_____

Team members sign on these lines.

This section completed by adult Team members.

My Team has learned a lot about how to respond to a bullying attempt. For example, the adult members of My Team have learned:

1. _____

2. _____

3. _____

My Team is working to keep our school and neighborhood safe and comfortable for all students. They are:

1. _____

2. _____

3. _____

This section completed by _____

My Team has learned a lot about how to respond to a bullying attempt. I have learned three steps to responding to a bullying attempt.

STEP 1 is: _____

STEP 2 is: _____

STEP 3 is: _____

My Team and I have learned the three steps to respond to a bullying attempt. Now, we can work together to fill in the thought, talk, and arrow symbols on page 118.

People are learning about bullying all over the world. Some people learn by completing workbooks and practicing. All people learn by working together. Look at what My Team has learned! Together, we will keep practicing. ■

CHAPTER 10

Understanding Adults

Adults Are Children Who Kept Getting Older

Many children learn about adults as they grow. I am a child. I am learning about adults. Understanding adults can make it easier to work and play with them.

Adults are older people. They were children long ago. They would still be children if they hadn't been here for so long. They couldn't help it; they didn't *decide* to be adults. It wasn't a *choice* that they made. They just kept growing older.

Sometimes, it helps to think of adults as really, really, really old children. Children like to have fun. So do adults. Children like to eat their favorite foods (and snacks that may not quite be food). So do adults. Children like to play. So do adults. Children have feelings. So do adults. Thinking of adults as really, really, really old children may help me to remember that each adult was once a child, like me. Adults may be easier to understand if I try to remember that they were once children, too.

Someday, I will be an adult. My turn as an adult is on its way—it's closer each day. Until then, I will try to remember that adults were children once, too. This may make adults a little easier for me to understand. ■

Learning to Respect Adults

Adults were here before me. Their birth dates came before mine.

It's important for children to understand that adults *are adults*. Adults have been here a long time. Adults have read more, studied more, and learned more. For this reason, adults make most of the decisions. That's Life on Planet Earth.

Sometimes, children wish that they could make adult decisions. Adults were once children who wished that at times, too. Now that they *are* adults, they've learned how difficult it can be to make decisions. Understanding *this* may make it easier for children to respect adults and the decisions that they make.

I am a child. I am learning about adults. Adults have been here a long time. They have a lot of experience. They know a lot. I will try to respect adults, and the decisions that they make. ■

The New Social Story™ Book, 15th Anniversary Edition
© by Carol Gray, Future Horizons, Inc.

Do Adults Know Everything?

To children, it may seem like adults know everything. Adults know how to get ready in the morning. They know how to drive. Most adults know enough to get through each day without having to go to a book or the Internet for help.

To children, it may seem like adults always know what to do. The truth is, sometimes adults get confused. They may make a wrong turn while driving or say, "Hi Evelyn!" to Ellen. They may have a problem and not know how to solve it. Most of the time, this is okay. All people get confused at times.

Adults don't know everything. Most adults do know where to find the information that they need. They know where to get help. Knowing where to get information, or how to get help, takes practice. Some adults are better at it than others.

Sometimes it may seem like adults know everything. The truth is, adults don't know everything. This is okay. ■

Why Moms and Dads Raise Children

Moms and dads raise children because they are well equipped to do it. In this case, *well equipped* means that they have what they need to complete the task.

There's a lot to know about caring for babies. Moms and dads know how to keep babies safe, feed them, and change their diapers and clothing. Moms and dads know when to put babies down for a nap, too. Moms and dads know how to care for babies.

There's a lot to know about caring for little children. Moms and dads know how to keep little children safe, feed them, and teach them to use toilets and bathtubs. Moms and dads know when to say "yes" or "no." They know how to read bedtime stories. Moms and dads know how to care for little children.

The New Social Story™ Book, 15th Anniversary Edition
© by Carol Gray, Future Horizons, Inc.

There's a lot to know about caring for older children. Moms and dads know how to keep older children safe, and how to get them to school and to other activities. Moms and dads know enough to decide what's okay, and what's not. Moms and dads know how to care for older children.

Moms and dads love their children. A lot. Love is very, very important in raising a child.

Grandparents know a lot about children, too. Years ago, they raised the moms and dads of today. They know how to love and how to raise children. But, because grandparents are a little older, they may get tired sooner. Sometimes, grandparents run out of stamina. *Stamina* is having enough energy and strength to keep going. Often, parents have more stamina than grandparents.

Moms and dads raise children because they are well equipped to do it. In this case, *well equipped* means that they have what they need to complete the task. ■

The New Social Story™ Book, 15th Anniversary Edition
© by Carol Gray, Future Horizons, Inc.

Adults Make Many Big Decisions

Adults make many decisions. Some people think that the biggest decisions are those that are made for other people. Moms and dads are adults. They make many decisions for their children. Teachers are adults. They make a lot of the decisions for their students.

As children grow, they make more decisions for themselves. Babies don't make many decisions, toddlers make a few more, preschoolers make a few more, and so on. Teenagers make more decisions than they ever did before, but not as many as they will make as adults.

Adults make many big decisions every day. Adults decide when it's okay for their children to have snacks or candy. They decide whether it's okay to allow their children to play computer games before homework is done. Teachers decide the best way to help students learn. The list of big decisions that adults make is very, very, very long.

Children may be able to help in decision-making. Sometimes, being quiet while adults think is helpful. Once in a while, children are asked for their ideas before a decision is made. For example, parents may ask their children where they would like to go for a vacation. When an adult makes a big decision, it's really helpful if children respect it.

Each day, adults make many big decisions for other people. Children may be able to help. ■

It May Not Be Fun but It Has to Be Done

I am learning about responsibility. Responsibility is completing activities that may not be fun, but have to be done.

There are activities that are fun. Many people think that watching a good movie is fun. **List A** is my list of three fun activities and why I like to do them. An adult may help.

LIST A: FUN ACTIVITIES

1. _____

I like this activity because _____

2. _____

I like this activity because _____

3. _____

I like this activity because _____

There are tasks that may not be fun—but have to be done. Many people think taking out the garbage is not fun. It has to be done or our home would smell like garbage. **List B** has lines to write three tasks that are not fun and why they have to be done.

LIST B: MAY NOT BE FUN BUT HAVE TO BE DONE TASKS

1. _____

It has to be done because _____

2. _____

It has to be done because _____

3. _____

It has to be done because _____

Sometimes, parents decide that children need to complete tasks from List B, before choosing activities from List A. This is an adult decision to make. It's also called teaching children *responsibility*.

I am learning to be responsible. When an adult decides a task has to be done, I will try to complete it before my activities in List A. ■

The New Social Story™ Book, 15th Anniversary Edition
© by Carol Gray, Future Horizons, Inc.

It Was Fun but Now We're Done

There are times when adults start a fun activity with children. There are also times when children find a fun thing to do on their own.

All fun activities end. Adults are used to having fun activities end. So they often handle it better than children. Little by little, children learn to end fun activities, too.

It is helpful to know when a fun activity needs to end. So, an adult may say, "In a few minutes, we have to put the toys away." This means playtime will end soon, but not now.

A few minutes pass. Then, an adult may say, "It was fun, but now we're done." This is a special sentence. It means that the fun activity ends now. It's time to put things away. It's time to go to another activity or task.

Sometimes, children think, *There will be another time for fun*. This helps them to stay calm and cooperative. They are right, too. There will be another fun time.

When I hear the special sentence, "It was fun, but now we're done," I will try to think of fun times to come. When a fun activity ends, I will try to stay calm and cooperative. ■

Please Hurry Up!

Parents often say, "Hurry up!" What might a parent be thinking? At different times of the day, what might 'hurry up' mean?

On a school day morning, 'hurry up' may mean *I don't want you to be late* … or … *please move faster as you get ready for school!*

Once in a while, 'hurry up' may mean finishing an activity in another way, like finishing a piece of toast in the car instead of at the kitchen table.

At home during free time, 'hurry up' may mean *come now*. It's time to leave an activity until later.

Sometimes parents say, "Hurry up!" Knowing what 'hurry up' means may make it easier to follow their request. ■

Permission

Children have many ideas. They have ideas about things they would like to do. A child's idea may be an adult's decision to make. When this happens, children need to ask for permission.

Permission is something that adults give to children. It's not a *thing* like a toy or chocolate. Permission is an okay to go ahead with an idea. Sometimes children get the permission that they need, other times they don't.

Here are two examples:

Antoine has an idea. He wants to take Jasper, his hamster, outside. Antoine's idea is his mom's decision to make. So Antoine asks his mom, "May I take Jasper outside?" Antoine's mom says, "Not right now." *Not right now* means, *No, not at this time.* Jasper the hamster stays inside.

Brooklyn wants to pick flowers. She asks her dad, "May I pick a flower from our garden?" Her dad says, "Sure." *Sure* means, *It's okay for Brooklyn to pick one flower.* Picking more than one flower may be a problem, because Brooklyn got her dad's permission to pick only one flower.

Sometimes when children ask for permission, the answer means *no*. Other times when children ask for permission, the answer means *yes*.

Permission is needed when a child has an idea, and it's an adult's decision to make. Sometimes children get the permission that they need, other times they don't. Either way, that's Life on Planet Earth! ■

The New Social Story™ Book, 15th Anniversary Edition
© by Carol Gray, Future Horizons, Inc.

Many Adults Like to Say "Yes"

Children have many ideas. They have ideas about things they would like to do. A child's idea may be an adult's decision to make. When this happens, children need to ask for permission.

Children may be surprised to learn that most adults like to say "yes" whenever they can. For many adults, giving permission and saying "yes" is fun. It's definitely more fun than saying "no." Long ago, when adults were children, they had to ask for permission. They remember how fun it was when adults said "yes" to them. They want to be fun like that, now.

Still, adults may decide to say "no." It's their decision to make. They may wish they could say "yes." But, they are adults. They've learned a lot. It's an adult's job to think and make the best decision that they can. This is why they may say "no."

Children have many ideas. Some of them need permission. For many adults, saying "yes" is fun. As adults, though, it's their job to think and make the best decision. Once in a while, the best decision isn't "yes"; it's "no." ■

The New Social Story™ Book, 15th Anniversary Edition
© by Carol Gray, Future Horizons, Inc.

Three Ways to Say "Yes"

Children have many ideas. They have ideas about things they would like to do. A child's idea may be an adult's decision to make. When this happens, children need to ask for permission.

An adult may say *yes*, without saying "yes." This may be a little confusing for children.

Sometimes, an adult will say, "Sure!" *Sure* is a definite *yes*. The adult is *very sure* that it's okay to give permission. The adult feels confident giving permission. It may also mean that permission in this case was not needed. Here's an example:

Jake: "Dad, may I do my homework now?"

Dad: "Sure!"

Other times, an adult will say, "Okay." *Okay* means *yes*. *Okay* may mean, *Yes this time, but not every time*. The adult feels comfortable giving permission. Here's an example:

Jake: "Dad, may Andrew and I do our homework together?"

Dad: "Okay."

Another way that adults often say yes is, "Okay, I guess," or, backwards, "I guess it's okay." This means, *Yes, but there is a good reason to say no*. The adult feels a little uncomfortable giving permission. This is why children often act fast when an adult says, "Okay, I guess."

Jake: "May I watch one television show before starting my homework?"

Dad, "Okay, I guess."

When children have ideas and ask for permission, adults may say *yes*. How they say yes can be a little confusing. Learning what adults mean when they say, "Sure," "Okay," or "Okay, I guess," can help. It's a clue to what adults may be thinking and feeling, too. ▪

The New Social Story™ Book, 15th Anniversary Edition
© by Carol Gray, Future Horizons, Inc.

If the Answer Is "No": A Story of Hope for Children

I have many ideas. I have ideas about things I would like to do. My idea may be an adult's decision to make. When this happens, it's important for me to try to ask for permission. Sometimes the adult will say "no." If the answer is no, there may be hope.

Sometimes, when an adult says "no," it also means, *I'm too tired to do that now*. There's hope! Maybe tomorrow it will be okay.

Sometimes, when an adult says "no," it also means, *That isn't safe*. There's hope! Maybe it can be made safer for me.

Sometimes, when an adult says "no," it also means, *Later the answer will be yes*. There's hope! Later almost always comes.

Sometimes, when an adult says "no," it also means, *We don't have enough money to buy that*. There's hope! Maybe we can save some money to buy it someday.

Sometimes, when an adult says "no," it means, *No, I will never allow that*. There's hope! The world is full of other things to do.

When adults have to say "no," they really love it when children try to stay calm. That way, the answer is "no" but everything else is still okay. And, they are more likely to say "yes" to another idea.

I have many ideas. Sometimes the answer will be "no." I will try to think, *There's hope!* and stay calm. ▪

The New Social Story™ Book, 15th Anniversary Edition
© by Carol Gray, Future Horizons, Inc.

CHAPTER 11

Home

Moving to a New Home

My family is moving to a new home. This is our moving plan, in three big steps:

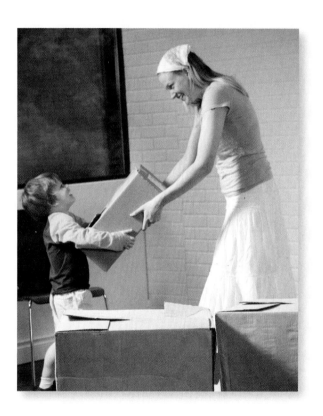

- Pack our furniture, and put other things in moving boxes.

- Take our furniture and boxes to the new home.

- Put our furniture and other things into the new home.

I am moving to a new home. I may pack some of my toys and things. This is my moving plan in three big steps:

- Pack. We'll put most of my toys and other things in moving boxes.

- Move. We'll take the boxes to the new home.

- Unpack. We'll put my toys and things in my home.

It's good to have a moving plan. My family and I have a plan for our move to a new home. ■

In Fletcher's Family, Who Knows What?

Fletcher knows a lot. He knows a LOT about dinosaurs. He knows a lot about his family, too. His father builds houses. His mother is a dentist. Fletcher's older sister, Emma, writes in her journal every day.

Someone in Fletcher's family knows how to build a garage. Guess who?

Someone in Fletcher's family knows a lot about cavities in teeth. Guess who?

Someone in Fletcher's family knows where to find the key to Emma's journal. Guess who?

Fletcher knows a lot about what the people in his family do. That gives him clues so he can guess *who* knows *what*! ∎

The New Social Story™ Book, 15th Anniversary Edition
© by Carol Gray, Future Horizons, Inc.

The Truth about Messes

My family lives in a home. We eat, take baths, sleep, get dressed, play, and work there. Sometimes, we make a mess.

When we eat, pots, pans, and plates get dirty. This can make a mess.

When we get ready for bed, we take off dirty clothes, put on pajamas, brush teeth, find bedtime stories, and find Slowmo, my turtle. This can make a mess.

When we sleep, the sheets get rumpled and our pajamas sometimes end up on the floor in the morning. It's starting to get messy already!

When we get dressed, things can get messy, too.

My family loves to play. That can really make a mess!

Sometimes Mom and Dad go outside to "clean up the yard. " Uh oh—does that get messy, too?

There's one true thing about messes: A mess is a mess until someone cleans it up.

A person might sit there, and look at a mess, and hope it will go away. Without help from that person, the mess will stay.

The truth about messes is that only people can make them go away. ■

Restating with Respect at Home

I am learning about respect. Respect helps everyone in my family feel important, comfortable, and safe. Talking respectfully to parents is a skill. It takes practice.

Sometimes, children make mistakes with respect. A child may use a disrespectful tone of voice or words. Talking disrespectfully to a parent is a mistake.

Parents want their children to feel comfortable and happy, and to use respect with others. If my brothers, my sisters, or I make a mistake with respect, my parents say, "Restate with respect, please."

"Restate with respect" gives us an important second chance. It gives us a chance to think. Next, we try to say it again with a calm voice and cooperative words. We try to say the same thing, but with respect.

If my mom or dad says to me, "Restate with respect, please," that means that I have made a mistake with respect. I will try to think and say it again using a calm voice and cooperative words. I will try to say it again with respect.

Many children make mistakes with respect. With practice, they learn how to talk to their parents with respect. ■

The New Social Story™ Book, 15th Anniversary Edition
© by Carol Gray, Future Horizons, Inc.

What Is a Babysitter?

My name is Joseph. Sometimes I have a babysitter. A babysitter is a person who takes care of babies and children.

Moms and dads ask a babysitter to come. They try to choose a babysitter who will take good care of their children when they cannot be home.

The babysitter comes before the parents leave. When the parents get back, the babysitter leaves.

Sometimes, I may go to the babysitter's house to stay until Mom or Dad comes back for me. This is okay. My mom and dad go to do other things. Whatever they do, they know where I am, and how to get there from anywhere.

Sometimes I have a babysitter. A babysitter is a person who takes care of me when my parents are away. ■

My Babysitter Knows about Me

I have many babysitters. They read this story about me. They know about me.

My babysitter knows that I like Thomas the Tank Engine™.

My babysitter knows that I sleep with Herbie the Elephant.

My babysitter knows where Herbie the Elephant is.

My babysitter knows the food that I like, and how to make it.

My babysitter knows that my favorite bedtime stories are in the elephant bookcase that Dad made.

My babysitter knows that the light in the hallway stays on.

My babysitter knows to leave the vacuum in the closet.

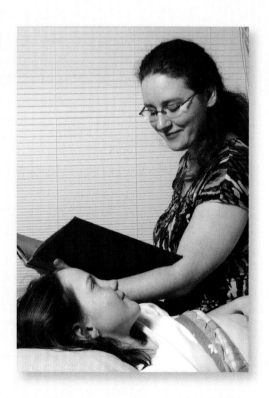

My babysitter knows all of these things and more. She knows how to take care of me until Mom and Dad are home again. ∎

The New Social Story™ Book, 15th Anniversary Edition
© by Carol Gray, Future Horizons, Inc.

CHAPTER 12

Community

Moving to a New Community

My name is Mason. I live in Shelton, Connecticut. My dad got a job in Garretson, South Dakota. My family is moving to a new home in Garretson.

I have never been to Garretson, South Dakota. My mom and dad have been to Garretson twice. They went once to look for a new home. They went another time to buy our home. They took many photos. Those photos are in my *Moving to Garretson Book.*

In Garretson, we'll do many of the errands and activities that we do now. We'll do them in and around Garretson, South Dakota.

I go to Lafayette Elementary School. In Garretson, I will go to Garretson Elementary School. I have photos of both of these schools in my book.

I get my hair cut at Rich and Ben's Hair Styling. In Garretson, I will get my hair cut at Brandon Plaza Barbers. I have photos of both of these barber shops in my book.

My family gets groceries at the Beechwood Supermarket. In Garretson, we can get groceries at Garretson Food Center. I have photos of both of these grocery stores in my book.

My name is Mason. Soon I will be living in Garretson, South Dakota. I will be going to school and getting my hair cut there. My mom and dad will buy groceries there. Garretson will be my new community. ■

The Up Escalator

In our community, people share the up escalators. An escalator is a moving set of stairs. An escalator is a good way to move people from one floor to another.

On a staircase, people move up from one step to the next. On an up escalator, people choose a step and ride it to the top!

To be safe, it's important to hold the handrail. The handrail moves at the same speed as the step. This makes an up escalator comfortable and safe for people to use.

Here's how to use an up escalator:

* Walk slowly to the bottom of the escalator.

* Pause just a little to decide which empty step to ride.

* Place a hand on the handrail next to that step.

* Look down, step with one foot, then the other, onto that step. This may be a big step.

* Ride up. To ride safely, stay on the same step.

* As the top gets closer, keep holding the handrail.

* At the top, the step begins to slowly flatten as it slides away under the landing. When this happens, let go of the handrail and walk off.

The New Social Story™ Book, 15th Anniversary Edition
© by Carol Gray, Future Horizons, Inc.

Most escalators are wide enough for two people to share a step. Sometimes I may have my own step. Other times, my mom, dad, brother, sister, or someone else that I know may ride with me.

Once in a while, an up escalator may be very, very busy. There are people waiting to use the escalator, and people on almost every step. When this happens, I may be told to share a step. At the top, it will be important to walk a few extra steps before stopping. This will leave enough room for other people to get off of the escalator.

The people in my community safely try to share the up escalators. I will try to safely share the up escalators, too. ■

Eating at the Food Court

My family is going to the mall. We may eat at the food court. The food court is a big area with many food vendors. Food vendors are small fast food restaurants. There is one big area where people can sit and eat. People choose a vendor, buy food, and then sit and eat at an open table.

People who work there work fast. They ask questions fast. They fill orders fast. They like it when customers make choices fast, too.

When a family eats at the food court, each person may choose their favorite vendor, and then eat together at the same table. Or, a family may decide to use one food vendor. It's my parents' decision to make.

Once my family decides which vendor or vendors to use, we may follow these steps to get our food:

1. Get in line. We may be first. If there are other people in a line before us, they will be ordering their food before us. If the person in front of us glances at us quickly, it may mean that we are standing too close. It's hard to know for sure. Whether or not this is the case, taking a step back may help.

The New Social Story™ Book, 15th Anniversary Edition
© by Carol Gray, Future Horizons, Inc.

2. Order food. To know when to order food, it helps to watch the person taking the orders closely. When it is our turn to order, that person may glance at us. He may also say something very fast. For example, he may say something like, "And for you?" or "Okay." This, that glance, and being next in line means that it is time for us to order.

3. Place food on tray. Parents can help with this.

4. Choose a place to sit. My mom or dad may already be at our table.

At the mall, my family may eat at the food court. ■

This Place Is Busy!

There are stores and restaurants in my community. Sometimes, they get busy. There are clues that a place is busy. A place may be busy if:

- There are a lot of people.

- People have to move slower than they would like to.

- To walk around, people have to stop to let others get where they are going.

- There are one or more long lines of people.

- There are many noises, and they are not just voices.

- My mom isn't smiling as much.

- Someone I am with says, "This place is busy!"

Some people enjoy busy places. Others do not. When parents enter a busy place, they may decide to stay. Or, they may decide to come back later or on another day. This is because it's hard for some parents to stay calm and happy in a busy place.

If a place is busy, it may change our plans. This is okay. Finding another time, when a place is less busy, may make it more fun to visit there.

When we are in the community, we may go to a busy place. We may stay, or we may come back later or another day. ■

CHAPTER 13

School

Is Today a School Day?

I go to school on school days. Mondays, Tuesdays, Wednesdays, Thursdays, and Fridays are often school days. Sometimes, though, my school will close.

There are many vacation days during the year. Some vacations are long, and others are short. Vacation days are written on the school calendar.

There are other special days when my school may be open for teachers, and closed for students. These are called teacher training or work days. They are usually written on the school calendar.

In the winter, it may snow a lot, or there may be ice. If it's very unsafe or difficult for cars or buses to get around, my school will close. It's called a *snow day*. People expect a few snow days in the winter, but snow days are not listed on the school calendar. That's because no one knows for sure when snow will close my school. My parents watch the local news to learn about snow days.

Sometimes, it may be confusing if today or tomorrow is a school day. Parents can help. Parents are very interested in school days. They know how to use the school calendar and the local news.

I go to school on school days. Sometimes, my school will be closed. ■

Absent Today? This Is Okay.

I am absent from school today. My parents say it's okay.

There are many reasons why a child may be absent. A child may be absent from school if:

- He is sick and needs to be home.

- He needs to go to the doctor or the dentist.

- His family is on a trip.

- There are other reasons a child may be absent, too.

When a child is absent, it is okay. The teacher will help him get his assignments, so that he can finish his schoolwork.

Today, I am absent because _____.
This is okay. My teacher will tell me about my assignments. That way, I will be able to finish my schoolwork.

Tomorrow I may be back in school, or I may be absent again. Mom and Dad can answer my questions about when I will be going back to school. ■

The New Social Story™ Book, 15th Anniversary Edition
© by Carol Gray, Future Horizons, Inc.

An Appointment on a School Day

Sometimes students have an appointment. An appointment may be during the school day. Once in a while I may have to leave school for an appointment.

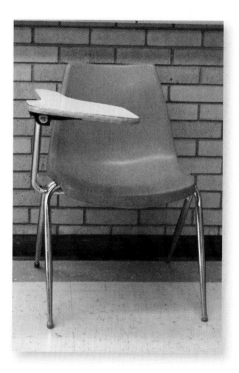

When I leave school for an appointment, the school remains open. The teachers and students stay for the rest of the school day.

It's okay if a student misses an assignment or activity because of an appointment. Teachers and parents can help. I may complete assignments or work that is missed at another time.

I may go to an appointment and return to school the same day. Or, I may return to school on another day. Either way is okay. My parents and teacher know my schedule when there is an appointment and when I will return to school. Leaving school for an appointment is okay. ■

When My Teacher Is Somewhere Else

My name is Andrea. My teacher's name is Mrs. Smith. Most school days, Mrs. Smith teaches the class. Sometimes, she has to be somewhere else.

Teachers get sick. Mrs. Smith may be sick. She may need to stay home.

Teachers go to teacher workshops. Mrs. Smith may go to a teacher workshop.

Many teachers have children, and their children get sick. Mrs. Smith has triplets. One of her triplets may be sick, so she needs to stay home.

We have a substitute teacher when Mrs. Smith needs to be somewhere else for the day. This is okay. Mrs. Smith will return to our class as soon as she can. ■

On a Substitute Teacher Day

Today my class has a substitute teacher. It's a substitute teacher day. This means that Mrs. Parker is not here. The substitute teacher is here. His name is Mr. McCuen. Some students may act differently.

On a substitute teacher day, many students work and play as they usually do. There are some students, though, who may talk more, get out of their seats more, break classroom rules more, and work less. They make mistakes that they don't usually make.

Many students want to help Mr. McCuen. If all the students in my class act like they do with Mrs. Parker, this will be most helpful. This probably won't happen today, though. There are some students who may not want to be most helpful to Mr. McCuen. There are other things that they want to do more.

Mr. McCuen knows about students who act differently when they have a substitute teacher. He expects some students to make that mistake. It's Mr. McCuen's job to make decisions about what to do. He's in charge of all students. He's in charge of students who may not be working as they usually do, too.

On a substitute teacher day, it's helpful if students work and play like they usually do. That's a good choice that helps the substitute teacher and other students, too. Some students may make another choice. The substitute teacher decides what to do about them. ■

Class Schedules

My name is Caitlyn. I am in Mrs. Jones class. Our class has a schedule.

Mrs. Jones made our class schedule. It is a plan for our class. It lists what we do on *most* school days.

Sometimes, Mrs. Jones will decide to follow another plan. The schedule will list an activity, and we will do another activity instead. This is okay. When this happens, Mrs. Jones will tell us about the new plan. We may follow the posted schedule tomorrow.

Most of the time, our class schedule matches what Mrs. Jones tells us to do. Sometimes, we'll have another plan. When this happens, I will try to do what Mrs. Jones tells us to do. ▪

The New Social Story™ Book, 15th Anniversary Edition
© by Carol Gray, Future Horizons, Inc.

The Truth about Our Class Schedule

My name is Hailey. I am in Mrs. Carlson's class. Our class has two schedules.

A schedule is a planned list of times and activities. One lists our special classes each week, and the times that we plan to start and finish them. Art and gym are on that schedule. The other lists our subjects each day, and the times that we plan to start and finish them. Math, journal time, and science are on that schedule.

The truth about schedules is that they are not people. Schedules don't know anything. A schedule is paper with words on it. It's a plan that stays the same, posted high on the wall so that everyone can see it.

Mrs. Carlson knows a lot. Sometimes, she knows the planned schedule won't work for our class. So, she tells my class what we will do. Here's another truth about our class schedule: At any time, Mrs. Carlson can *overrule* the schedule.

In this case, *overrule* means that Mrs. Carlson has more power than the pieces of paper with our schedules. If she tells us to do something different from the schedule, we try to do it.

Here's an example of how that works. Last week, the class schedule listed art next, at one o'clock (1:00). Mrs. Carlson told everyone to put their math books away. All of a sudden, the fire drill sounded. Mrs. Carlson said, "Okay, fire drill. Line up at the door. We're going outside." She overruled our weekly schedule, just like that. The fire drill took so long that art was cancelled.

A posted schedule is paper with a plan listed on it. At our school, most of the time, teachers have more power than schedules on paper. That's the truth about schedules. ■

The New Social Story™ Book, 15th Anniversary Edition
© by Carol Gray, Future Horizons, Inc.

Learning about Directions at School

Sometimes teachers, or other school staff, tell students what to do. They give students directions.

Directions help students work, learn, and play together. Directions help to keep students safe, too.

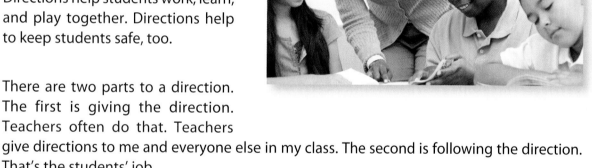

There are two parts to a direction. The first is giving the direction. Teachers often do that. Teachers give directions to me and everyone else in my class. The second is following the direction. That's the students' job.

I am learning about directions at school. Directions help a class work, learn, and play safely together. ■

The Big Yellow Everyone Look and Listen Sign

My name is Elijah. I go to school. Mr. Carter is my teacher. He has a big, yellow sign.

This is The Big Yellow Everyone Look and Listen Sign. It's important. It means, *Everyone try to look at Mr. Carter. Everyone try to listen to Mr. Carter, too.* Most of the time, Mr. Carter just calls it the Look and Listen Sign. It's his sign, so he can do that.

There are times when Mr. Carter is talking to me and everyone else. Many times, he's at the front of the room when this happens. He puts his Look and Listen Sign where everyone can see it. It means that this is a time for everyone to pay attention to him.

Mr. Carter puts up his sign when he is teaching. It's up when he teaches us math, reading, writing, spelling, science, and other subjects. It's up when Mr. Carter tells us about a class assignment. It's up when he has directions for me and everyone else. It's up whenever he is talking to everyone in class at the same time.

This is the back of Mr. Carter's sign. There are times when Mr. Carter does not need everyone to listen to him. In my class, we have times when everyone is working. Mr. Carter may talk to another teacher or the principal. Sometimes Mr. Carter is talking to a few students, like a reading group. Or, he may come and talk just to me, but not anyone else. During those times, this side of the sign is up.

The Big Yellow Everyone Look and Listen Sign means, *Elijah and everyone else try to look at Mr. Carter, and listen to him, too.* It helps me to know when it is important for me to try to pay attention to Mr. Carter. ■

It's My Teacher's Decision

Teachers make many decisions for their class. A decision is a firm—and usually final—choice. Teachers make a lot of decisions, like who collects the lunch money and how to care for classroom pets. It's their job.

Teachers often make decisions about ideas from students. Asia has an idea. She wants to collect the lunch money today. Asia's teacher, Miss Capel, decides who collects the lunch money. Asia asks Miss Capel, "May I collect the lunch money today?"

"That would be fine," says Miss Capel. "That would be fine" is a *yes decision*. This *yes decision* means that Asia may collect the lunch money today.

Christopher has an idea. He wants to let Angel, the hamster, out of her cage. Miss Capel decides when Angel is out of her cage. Christopher asks Miss Capel, "May I let Angel out of her cage?"

"Not right now, Christopher," says Miss Capel. "Not right now" is a *no decision*. This *no decision* means that Angel, the hamster, will be in her cage.

Teachers make many decisions each day. My teacher makes decisions, too. Sometimes, my teacher may make a *yes decision*. Other times my teacher may make a *no decision*. Making decisions is a part of my teacher's job. ■

The New Social Story™ Book, 15th Anniversary Edition
© by Carol Gray, Future Horizons, Inc.

My Place in Line

It's my teacher's job to give my class directions. It's our job to try to follow those directions.

Sometimes, many students move from one place to another. To walk safely, and to allow other groups to walk through the hall at the same time, it's important to try to walk in a line.

Many students like to be first in line. The teacher decides which student is first in the line. Sometimes, I will be the first student in line. Most of the time, another child will be first. When this happens, I will be at another place in the line. This helps the teacher give each student a chance to be first.

My teacher decides which student is first in the line. Once in a while, I will be first in line. Most of the time, another student will be first in line. That's how lines work at my school. That's Life on Planet Earth. ◼

Learning about Lines at School

I am learning about lines at school. Knowing how to use school lines is important.

On the playground, many children may want to use the slide. As one child slides, the other children wait in a line for their turn. Keeping the line pretty straight makes it easy to know who slides next.

At the drinking fountain, many children may want a drink of water. As one child drinks the other children wait in a line for their turn. Keeping the line pretty straight makes it easy to know who drinks next.

In the cafeteria, many children want to get their lunch. As a few children get lunch, the other children wait in a line for their turn. Keeping the line pretty straight makes it easy to know who gets their lunch next.

Lines help children share the playground, drinking fountain, and cafeteria safely and fairly. Lines help children in other places at school, too! Keeping lines pretty straight makes it easy to know who's 'next'. I will try to practice what I am learning about lines when taking turns at schools, and other places, too! ■

Lining up at the Door

There are many students at my school. Sometimes my teacher tells the students to 'line up at the door.' Lining up at the door usually means we will all be walking to another place.

When we 'line up at the door' we try to stand one student behind the other. One student is first. A second student stands behind the first. A third student stands behind the second. Except for the first student, each student stands behind another student in the line.

The line stands for a few moments. Sometimes it may feel a little crowded or squishy. This often happens when many students stand in a small space. Sometimes children tuck in their shirts or scratch their heads. Sometimes students just wiggle a little. They may touch students around them as they do these things.

My teacher may ask us to 'stand still.' This makes standing in a line more comfortable and gets us ready to walk.

When my teacher tells us to line up at the door, it helps to know what it means and what to expect. ■

Will I be First in Line?

Sometimes my class forms a line. Once in a while, I will be first. Most of the time I will be in another place in the line.

When my teacher says, "Please line up at the door," we form a line. One student is first, one child is second, another is third, and so on. Each student has a place in line. We use our line to walk safely to another place.

I like to be first in line. Once in a while and what may seem like almost never, I will be the first student in the line. When this happens, the teacher is right in front of me.

Most students want to be first in line, just like me. To be fair, we take turns. That's why most of the time another student is first in line. When this happens one of my classmates will be in front of me. This is okay.

Sometimes my class forms a line. Once in a while, I will be first. Most of the time one of my classmates will be first. This is fair and okay. ■

The New Social Story™ Book, 15th Anniversary Edition
© by Carol Gray, Future Horizons, Inc.

Learning about Respect at School

Respect is being careful and thoughtful with other people. People show respect with kind words and actions. Respect helps everyone feel welcome, comfortable, and safe.

Teachers and students try to show respect at school. Here are some examples:

- *Respect* is using kind words and actions.

- *Respect* is carefully helping another student.

- *Respect* is sharing.

Respect is being careful and thoughtful with other people. At school, respect helps everyone to feel welcome, comfortable, and safe. ■

Using Respect at School

Respect is being careful and thoughtful with other people. People show respect with kind words and actions. Respect helps everyone feel welcome, comfortable, and safe.

Teachers and students try to show respect at school. Here are some examples:

- Respect is using kind words and actions. When Miss Jacobs works with her fifth graders, she often uses a kind voice and a smile.

- Respect is carefully helping another student. Samantha dropped the envelope with her book-fair money in the hallway. Jose saw it fall. He picked up the envelope and said, "Here, Samantha. You dropped this."

- Respect is sharing. Aidan needed a blue marker. Jenna had one. "Here," Jenna said to Aidan, "You may use mine."

- "Thank you, Jenna," said Aidan. Saying "thank you" shows respect, too!

- Respect is working quietly when others are trying to think, or finish their assignments. Tristan finished his work first. He read a book silently until the test was over.

Respect is being careful and thoughtful with other people. At school, respect helps everyone feel welcome, comfortable, and safe. ■

Talking to a Teacher with Respect

Students learn to talk to teachers with respect. Respect is being careful and thoughtful with another person. When students talk with respect, they use a calm voice and kind words.

It's easiest for students to talk with respect when they're feeling happy, calm, or comfortable.

Sometimes, a student may have a problem, or feel frustrated or angry. *Frustration* and *anger* are two negative feelings. Negative feelings are uncomfortable. They make it more difficult to talk with respect. It's important to learn how to keep negative feelings under control. That way, a student can talk with respect even when feeling uncomfortable.

Many students work hard to learn how to keep their feelings under control. With practice, many students discover that keeping feelings under control makes it easier to talk with respect. ■

Restating with Respect at School

I am learning about respect. Respect helps everyone feel welcome, comfortable, and safe. Learning to talk with respect to a teacher is a skill. Students need to think about, and practice, talking with respect. Sometimes, a student may make mistakes with respect. A student may use a disrespectful tone of voice or words with a teacher.

Talking disrespectfully to a teacher is a mistake. Teachers want students to do well, and to use respect with others. Whenever a student talks to my teacher, Mr. Westra, with a disrespectful tone of voice or words, Mr. Westra says, "Restate with respect, please."

"Restate with respect," gives students an important second chance. This gives students a chance to think and say it again with a calm voice and cooperative words. This gives students a chance say the same thing, but with respect.

If Mr. Westra says to me, "Restate with respect, please," that means that I have made a mistake with respect. I will try to think and say it again using a calm voice and cooperative words. I will try to say it again with respect.

Many students make mistakes with respect. With practice, they learn the skill of talking to teachers with respect. ■

The New Social Story™ Book, 15th Anniversary Edition
© by Carol Gray, Future Horizons, Inc.

When I Talk with Respect at School

I am learning to talk with respect. Talking with respect is using a calm, controlled voice with cooperative words. When working and playing with adults, classmates, and friends, talking with respect is very important. That way, everyone feels comfortable.

Adults in charge of me at school notice when I talk with respect. For example, at the book fair, there was a book that I really wanted. I did not have enough money. An adult told me to put the book back on the shelf. I was very disappointed, but I used cooperative words, saying, "Okay," with a calm voice.

Here are other respectful things that I have said at school:

_____

_____

_____

People notice when I talk with respect! They feel calm and comfortable when I use cooperative words and a calm voice. ▪

What Is Practice?

Students learn many important skills. Reading is a skill. Math, writing, and spelling are skills, too. Practice is one way that students learn.

Sometimes, teachers ask students to practice skills. *Practice* is carefully doing a skill over and over.

When students learn to add, they practice by solving many math problems.

When students learn to write, they practice making letters by writing each letter many times.

When students learn to spell a word, they practice spelling it correctly.

Practice helps students learn many important skills. ■

The New Social Story™ Book, 15th Anniversary Edition
© by Carol Gray, Future Horizons, Inc.

Mistakes Happen on the Way to Learning

Students often make mistakes. This is okay. Mistakes often happen on the way to learning.

Students often make mistakes when they learn to add or subtract. This is okay. Mistakes often happen on the way to learning math.

Students often make mistakes when they learn to write letters and words. This is okay. Mistakes often happen on the way to learning writing.

Students often make mistakes when they learn about plants, animals, rocks, or outer space. This is okay. Mistakes often happen on the way to learning science.

Students often make mistakes on the way to learning about other countries, their history, and their people. This is okay. Mistakes often happen on the way to learning geography, history, and social studies.

Mistakes often happen on the way to learning. I may make mistakes on the way to learning. This is okay. ■

Schoolwork is Practice

School is where I learn about many things for the first time. School is where I practice what I learn.

Practice is doing an exercise or activity over and over. Singers practice. Football players practice. Cooks practice. Musicians practice. Golfers practice. Students practice. They all practice to make skills easier and to improve their performance.

Many skills at school get easier and faster with practice. Reading new words is slower at first, easier and faster with practice. Solving addition or multiplication problems is slower at first, easier and faster with practice. Spelling new words is slower at first, easier and faster with practice.

Teachers make assignments to give students practice with new skills. That way, skills become easier and students are ready to learn new things. I will try to complete assignments to practice new skills. ■

The New Social Story™ Book, 15th Anniversary Edition
© by Carol Gray, Future Horizons, Inc.

That's Great!

WHAT TO DO WITH MISTAKES ON SCHOOLWORK

A mistake is an error. All students make mistakes. So, most students are not surprised to see them on their schoolwork. They may feel sad or disappointed, but not really surprised.

Expecting mistakes helps students prepare for the disappointment of seeing them on their corrected papers. Expecting mistakes helps many students stay calm, so they can think and handle any mistake well.

Sometimes, students are told to correct mistakes on schoolwork. That's one reason why most pencils have erasers. Students try to figure out what they did wrong. Then, they erase the mistake and make it right. That's one good way to handle a mistake.

Other times, it's difficult to figure out why an answer is wrong. Staying calm helps students do their best thinking. Sometimes, thinking a little longer helps a student correct the mistake. That's another great way to handle a mistake.

Often, there are times when students need help with a mistake. They try to figure out what they did wrong, and think a little longer, but still are confused by the mistake. So, they ask for help. Asking for help is another great way to handle a mistake.

I'm a student. I'm likely to make mistakes. I'm learning to expect them. That way, I may learn to be great at handling my mistakes! ■

Telling My Teacher about a Problem

Teachers and students talk about many things. They often talk about good news. They can also solve problems together.

Sometimes, a student may have a problem, or feel frustrated or angry. Telling the teacher can help. That way, the teacher will know there is a problem. Teachers want to help. They have a lot of ideas. Teachers can help to solve problems.

If I have a problem at school, telling the teacher may help. If I feel frustrated or angry, telling the teacher may help, too. My teacher has a lot of ideas. She can help to solve problems.

Teachers can help students solve problems and feel more comfortable again. ■

Staying Calm with Difficult Schoolwork

Students learn new ideas and skills at school. Sometimes learning is easy. Other times learning is more difficult, especially at first. This is okay.

When an assignment is difficult, staying calm is important. Staying calm helps students think better and stay smart.

Most students use a plan or action—a *strategy*—to stay calm.

Some students take a big, deep, slow breath. This helps them to keep their feelings in control.

Some students think about something nice to stay calm.

Other students 'self-talk'. They may think things like, *'I'm safe and okay'* or *'My teacher can help.'*

There are students may take a short break and return to work.

Teachers' know that feeling calm and comfortable at school is important. They can help me learn my own strategy to stay calm and in control. That way, I will be able to do my best work. ■

What if Schoolwork is Difficult? Teachers can Help.

Students learn new ideas and skills at school. Sometimes, learning is easy. Sometimes, learning is more difficult, especially at first. Adults can help.

Adults are children that grew up. They went to school. Some schoolwork was easy. Other schoolwork was difficult. Adults have learned skills that I am learning now.

Teachers and other adults can help children practice and learn new skills. A child may ask for help. That way, adults know help is needed.

There are many ways that adults help children learn. Sometimes adults help by explaining or demonstrating. Sometimes they help by telling children what to do, step by step.

Adults also help by asking questions. Questions help student's think and work through a problem or idea. The adults already knows the answer, but they want to help the student think of the answer for her/herself. Asking students questions is one way that adults teach.

When learning is difficult there are adults that can help. ■

What's My Teacher Thinking?

At school, my teacher is always thinking.

This teacher is giving directions. Let's guess. What might this teacher be thinking?

This teacher is correcting student work. Let's guess. What might this teacher be thinking?

This teacher is watching children play. Let's guess. What might this teacher be thinking?

This teacher is looking at the classroom schedule. Let's guess. What might this teacher be thinking?

At school, teachers are always thinking. ■

The New Social Story™ Book, 15th Anniversary Edition
© by Carol Gray, Future Horizons, Inc.

How to Make a Writing Box

Learning to write takes time and practice. Students have many wonderful ideas. A writing box keeps those ideas ready for writing!

A writing box begins as a shoebox, one shoebox for each student. Students may decorate their box, or leave it plain.

Each student's favorite items, like photos, toys, or other small objects, are placed in the box. These items transform a shoebox into a student's own Writing Box. The box is kept at school.

For many writing assignments, the items in the box may help students find a topic. Looking through the box, the student selects an item, an idea for a writing topic.

Sometimes, it helps to keep a selected item out while writing. A student may write what they remember about an item, or find interesting details in a photo. In this way, a writing box helps students develop their ideas.

Many students use writing boxes at school. It helps them to discover topics and develop their ideas. I may try to make a writing box for school, and maybe for home, too! ◼

How to Write a True Story

I am learning to use my writing box to write a true story. A true story describes something that really happened. Students often write true stories in journals. To learn to write a true story, I may try following these five steps.

STEP 1

A true story is about real people. They are the characters in a true story. The main character is the most important person in the story. I may be the main character in my true story. Or, I may write a true story about someone that I know. I will try to choose a main character for my story.

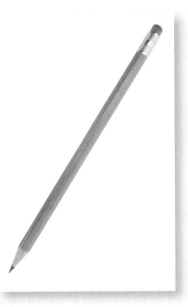

STEP 2

A true story often describes an experience. I have a writing box with photographs of real experiences. I may try choosing a photo to write about.

STEP 3

People who read my story want to know who is in the photo, and where the photo was taken. This makes a good beginning to my story. I will try to write a beginning to my story.

The New Social Story™ Book, 15th Anniversary Edition
© by Carol Gray, Future Horizons, Inc.

STEP 4

People who read my story want to know about what the people or animals in the photo are doing. This makes a good middle to my story. I will try to write a middle to my story.

STEP 5

People who read my story want to know about how my story ends. They want to know what happened last. My story needs an ending. I will try to write an ending to my story.

A true story is a story about something that really happened. Following these five steps may make it easier to write my story. I will try to write a story with a main character, and a beginning, middle, and ending. ■

A-Okay Ways to Finish My Work

My name is Brandon. I am an awesome student at Lincoln School. Most of the time, it is important that students finish their work.

ONE WAY

One way to finish work is to finish it all at one time. This means that a student starts it, works on it, and finishes it. Then, that student begins another activity.

STUDENTS OFTEN HAVE TO DO THEIR WORK ANOTHER WAY

A school schedule is full of many activities. Sometimes, it's best if students finish their work Another Way. Adults decide if it's okay to use another way.

To finish work Another Way:

- Students begin working, then they

- Go do something else, and

- Come back to finish it later.

Begin working.   Go do something else.   Come back to finish it later.

Most of the time, it's important for students to finish their work. There are two ways to finish work: One Way and Another Way. Each school day, adults decide which way is okay. ■

The New Social Story™ Book, 15th Anniversary Edition
© by Carol Gray, Future Horizons, Inc.

Good Questions for Small Group Projects

Questions are an important part of learning. When students work together, what is a good question?

Mr. Hailey's class is dividing into small groups. Each group will choose a city to study. What are good questions for this project?

A good question may make a suggestion and ask others for their ideas at the same time. One example is this: "I'd like to do our report on Columbus, Ohio. What other cities could we study?"

A good question may invite others to join in. One example is this: "Zachary, you went to San Diego. Would that be a good city to add to our list?"

A good question may show interest in what others are doing. One example is this: "Jackson, I loved the map you drew of downtown. Could you make a city map for our project?"

A good question may help add details to an idea. One example is this: "Jackson, what would you think about drawing a three-dimensional picture of one of the streets in our city, too?"

A good question may help students work things out. One example is this: "Jackson, Darla wants to draw the city map. What would you think if she does the map, and you do a three-dimensional drawing of one of the streets? That will save you time." Sometimes, help from an adult may be needed to find a solution.

A good question may seek help from others. One example is this: "I'd like to work on writing the report. But I'll need help. Who can help with that?"

When students work in small groups, a good question is one that helps students share ideas or solve problems. ■

An Emergency?

THE PEOPLE AT MY SCHOOL KNOW WHAT TO DO

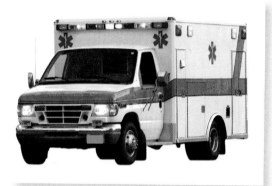

Once in a while, there may be an emergency at my school. An emergency is a dangerous, sometimes-unexpected situation. In an emergency, people need to act right away.

There are many kinds of school emergencies. Once, Kendra broke her arm when she fell on the playground. That was an emergency. Mr. Burns, our teacher, helped Kendra right away. He knew what to do. Kendra is okay now.

Another time, Nicholas in Miss Keyser's class was very sick. None of us expected that to happen. All morning Nicholas was fine. All of a sudden, he was sick. Miss Keyser got help right away. An ambulance took Nicholas to the hospital. Nicholas is okay now.

Fires and tornadoes are very big school emergencies. In these emergencies, *everybody* in the school needs to know what to do. Everyone has to act right away, at the same time. There has never been a fire at my school. There has never been a tornado, either. If there ever is a fire or tornado, though, everyone in my school knows what to do.

Once in a while there may be an emergency at my school. If there is, people in my school know what to do. ◼

What Is a Drill?

In an emergency, it's important for people to act right away. It's important for them to know what to do. A drill can help people be ready for a big emergency. What is a drill?

A drill is *practice* that is done the same, best way each time. Drills help people make fewer mistakes.

In a big emergency, it is very, very, very important for everyone to know what to do. This helps to keep everyone safe. For this reason, many people use drills to practice for big emergencies. Firemen, policemen, doctors, nurses, and the people in my school use drills to practice for emergencies.

A drill is practice that is done the same, best way each time. That way, in a big emergency everyone knows the best thing to do. People use drills to help them practice. That way, they are ready for big emergencies. ■

The New Social Story™ Book, 15th Anniversary Edition
© by Carol Gray, Future Horizons, Inc.

Why Principals Schedule Drills

Most school buildings are safe places. Once in a very long while, there may be a big emergency at my school. School fires and tornadoes are big emergencies. A few times each school year, our principal schedules drills for us to practice what to do if there is a fire or tornado.

A drill is practice that is done the same, best way each time. In an emergency, it's important to act right away. Knowing exactly what to do helps to keep people calm and safe. During a drill, everything is really safe and okay. That's the very best time to practice for an emergency.

Our principal schedules the drills. She knows when they will happen. Most people in our school do not know when there will be a fire or tornado drill. Not knowing when it will happen is part of the drill. Since fires and tornadoes are often unexpected, it's important to practice for them that way.

On a school day, there are many people at school. Someday, there may be a tornado or a fire at my school. It's important for each person to know what to do. This takes practice. So, principals schedule drills. ■

Fire Drills at School

School buildings are safe places. Once in a very long while, a fire may start in a school. If this happens, it's very important for everyone to calmly, quickly, and safely leave the building at the same time. This takes practice. So, principals schedule fire drills.

During a fire drill, everything in a school is safe and okay. That's the very best time to for teachers and students to practice leaving a school.

A drill is practice that is done the same, best way each time. In a fire drill, each class has their own route to leave the building. This keeps people from bumping into one another. If there ever was a fire, a special route helps everyone get out of the building calmly, quickly, and safely.

Once outside, each class has a special safe area. This is where they stop and count to make sure everyone is out of the building. Then they wait for the "all clear" signal to return to class.

There is usually more than one fire drill each school year. Each time, every class leaves the school the same way. They go to the same area outside of the building.

Most school buildings are safe all of the time. Once in a very long while, a fire may start in a school. Fire drills help teachers and students practice so that everyone knows how to leave the school calmly, quickly, and safely. ■

The New Social Story™ Book, 15th Anniversary Edition
© by Carol Gray, Future Horizons, Inc.

Why Schools Have Fire Alarms

Every school has a fire alarm. A fire alarm is a safety device. My school has a fire alarm.

A fire alarm makes a very special, loud and uncomfortable sound. This is to get everyone's attention. It is used to start a fire drill. It is also used if there is a fire anywhere in a building.

A fire alarm means leave the building now. Everyone in the school knows that when they hear it, it's time to leave the building and go to their safe area outside.

Fire alarms will always sound uncomfortable, like the one at my school. Knowing why they are made that way, and what they mean, doesn't make them any quieter. It does, though, help people understand why they are in every school. ■

About Tornado Drills

Most of the time, weather is safe for people. Once in a long while, there is severe weather. In severe weather, often people need to do special things to keep safe. A tornado is very severe weather.

There are many people in a school. If there is a tornado, it's important to get all of the people to the safest places in the school. Adults and children use tornado drills to practice moving to those places.

A tornado drill starts with a loud and unique alarm. That way, no one confuses it with another bell, like the one that ends recess. When adults and children hear the special alarm, they know it is time to practice moving to a safer place in the school.

In a tornado drill, there is no tornado. It's a time to practice moving to a safer place calmly and quickly. If there is a tornado someday, the same loud and unique noise will sound. When a tornado drill is over, returns to what they were doing before the drill or the next activity on their schedule.

My school will have tornado drills. We will practice what to do if there is a tornado. That way, if someday there is a tornado, we will all know what to do. ◾

Where Does Everyone Go?

The school day ends. Where does everyone go?

My teacher may stop at a grocery store before going home.

One student may go to a music lesson.

Another student may go to baseball practice.

Sometimes a few students may play together.

Or, a student may go home to rest and have free time.

When the school day ends, each person continues their day in their own way. ■

The New Social Story™ Book, 15th Anniversary Edition
© by Carol Gray, Future Horizons, Inc.

CHAPTER 14

Planet Earth

That's Life on Planet Earth

I live on Planet Earth. All people live on Planet Earth with me. It's our "home" planet. There are some experiences that almost all people have in common. These experiences are a part of life here, on Planet Earth.

People wake up. Sometimes they are happy to wake up. Other times they would like to be able to sleep longer. That's Life on Planet Earth.

People live in homes. Sometimes everything works, other times something needs to be fixed. That's Life on Planet Earth.

People often go places. Sometimes they arrive exactly on time. Sometimes they arrive late. Sometimes people arrive early. That's Life on Planet Earth.

People make mistakes. Sometimes they make big mistakes. Sometimes they make little mistakes. That's Life on Planet Earth.

For all Planet Earth people, there are likely to be:

- Times when they are happy to wake up, and other times they'd rather sleep

- Days when everything works, and other days when something needs to be fixed

- Times when they are on time, late, or early

- They will make big mistakes and little ones, too. That's Life on Planet Earth.

Because I am a Planet Earth person, there are likely to be:

- Times when I am happy to wake up, and other times I'd rather sleep

- Days when everything works, and other days when something needs to be fixed

- Times when I'm on time, late, or early

It's likely that I may make big mistakes and little ones, too. That's Life on Planet Earth. ■

The New Social Story™ Book, 15th Anniversary Edition
© by Carol Gray, Future Horizons, Inc.

I'm Taking a Flight

My name is Jordan. Mom and Dad told me that I will be taking a flight with them soon. That means that I will be riding in an airplane.

There's a lot to know about flying in an airplane. I have a set of stories to help.

I am riding on a plane soon. People will probably be saying to me, "Have a good flight!" ■

Who Are the Crew?

Every flight has a crew. Most crews have a pilot, co-pilot, and one or more flight attendants. They wear uniforms. That way, passengers know which people are members of the crew.

The pilot and co-pilot fly the plane. They have studied and practiced to learn how to fly a plane. The pilot and copilot work near the front of the plane in the cockpit. It's their job to fly the plane and to lead the crew.

Flight attendants work in the cabin of the airplane. They studied and practiced to learn how to keep passengers comfortable and safe. The cabin has a small kitchen, one or more bathrooms, and many seats for passengers.

The crew works to keep passengers comfortable and safe. ■

Who Are the Passengers on an Airplane?

Many airplanes carry passengers. A passenger is a person with a ticket to ride on the plane. A passenger may be a child, like me. Or, a passenger may be an older adult, like my grandparents. Sometimes, a baby or toddler is a passenger.

Passengers do not need to know how to fly a plane, or how to keep everyone safe. It's important, though, for passengers to listen to directions from the pilots and flight attendants. It's so important that there are laws about following directions on an airplane. This helps the pilot and flight attendants keep everyone safe.

I may be a passenger on a plane, too. If I am, I may see babies, toddlers, children, and adults who are passengers with me. We will all have a ticket to ride the plane! ▪

What Does "Going through Security" Mean?

Keeping passengers and crew safe on an airplane is very important. Going through security helps to find passengers or items that could be a problem on a flight. That's why all passengers and crew have to "go through security" before they get on an airplane.

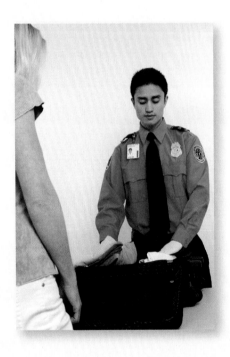

There are airport officers that help everyone go through security. These airport officers are friendly with people who cooperate and suddenly serious with people who don't. That's because they are helping people and looking for problem people and items, all at the same time.

Catching problems early is better than discovering them after the crew and passengers get on the plane. Going through security is one way to discover problems. Airport officers have a very important job. Cooperative passengers help everyone "go through security," so that they can get on their plane. ▪

The New Social Story™ Book, 15th Anniversary Edition
© by Carol Gray, Future Horizons, Inc.

Directions for Going through Security

Following directions when going through security is very important. Most people do not like to go through security. It's just something they have to do if they want to ride on a plane.

These are the directions for going through security:

- If there's a line of people at any point in security, wait for a turn.

- If airport officers tell you to do something that is not on this list, do it.

- Show your boarding pass and identification to the first officer.

- Put shoes and cases on the conveyer belt to go through the scanning machine.

- Place other things in the bins as directed.

- Walk through the short security tunnel.

- Put items back in their cases, put on shoes.

Following the directions for going through security helps the airport officers find problem passengers or items. This helps to keep everyone safe. ■

Moms, Dads, and Airport Security

Sometimes, moms and dads are serious or stressed when they go through security at an airport. It helps children to know why this happens, and what their parents may be thinking or feeling as they go through security.

First, it's a little harder for a family with children to go through security. Families have more stuff that they carry with them onto a plane. This stuff makes traveling with children easier and fun. It makes going through security a little stressful, though. Some items have to be unpacked and placed on the scanner. Moms and dads worry about getting everything through the scanner. They also worry about forgetting something when they repack everything afterwards. And, most important, they are keeping track of their children, too. They've a lot to do in a short time.

Second, especially if there's a long line, parents are hoping their children really cooperate and follow the rules. When moms and dads start thinking about the people who are waiting in line behind them, it adds to their stress. This is because they know others want to get through security quickly. Sometimes, moms and dads may try to get their children to move faster. Their children, though, may be distracted by interesting things, like the conveyer belt and the security scanner.

Families going through security are a little slower than others. Sometimes moms and dads may seem serious or stressed. Knowing why they feel this way is helpful information for their children. ■

The New Social Story™ Book, 15th Anniversary Edition
© by Carol Gray, Future Horizons, Inc.

What Airport Officers Say and Mean

Airport officers ask questions—or tell people what to do—as they go through security. Once in a while or maybe more than that, an airport officer may ask a question to tell someone what to do. This may be a little confusing. Airport officers do this because they want to be polite as they watch for problem items and people. This results in friendly questions without choices; questions that give a direction. Knowing about questions that are really directions helps passengers to do the right thing, at the right time.

Here are some examples:

- An airport officer may say, "May I see your boarding pass?" This means, *You must show me your boarding pass now.*

- An airport officer may say, "May I look in your bag?" This means, *I need to look in your bag. If you say "no," you may not be getting on the plane.*

- An airport officer may say, "Would you please remove your belt and walk through the scanner again?" This means, *Remove your belt and walk through the scanner.*

Airport officers try to be friendly while doing a very, very serious job. Knowing that this may cause them to use friendly questions to give no-choice directions helps everyone get through security more easily. ◼

Jet Way Lines May Be Slow at Times

Planes fly in and out of airports. Many times a jet way is used to connect an airplane to an airport. People walk in the jet way to get onto a plane. Sometimes, passengers need to stop and wait in the jet way. Knowing why this happens helps people stay calm.

Passenger airplanes have many seats. This gives each person a place to sit on the plane. It doesn't leave a lot of room for people to walk. When fifty, one hundred, or more people get on a plane, the aisle fills up very quickly. A line forms out into the jet way.

Meanwhile, other passengers are already in the airplane, getting settled into their seats. Sometimes they have to take off their coats, put their luggage away, or help another passenger. All of this takes time, especially when there are a lot of passengers.

Jet way lines can be slow at times. Jet way lines often stop, then move, then stop, then move. Even so, it is the fastest way to get many people with bags and luggage down one aisle and into their seats.

Most passengers would rather be in their seats than standing in a slow jet way line. They may feel a little uncomfortable or frustrated. It's important to try to stay calm. Sometimes thinking can help. Passengers may think, *This is what happens when two hundred people get on an airplane*, or, *The line will move again soon*, or, *Others will wait for me when I am getting settled into my seat*. Thinking to stay calm in a jet way is smart.

I may use a jet way to get onto a plane. If there are many people, the line may move slowly. The line of people, with me in it, may need to stop and wait now and then. This is okay. I will try to think to stay calm. This is smart for me, and helpful for the passengers around me. ■

Parents Are Important Passengers

Parents are important passengers. They help the pilot and flight attendants.

Parents are important adult passengers. They listen for directions, and help their children follow those directions.

That's why my mom or dad may tell me to wait to use the bathroom on the airplane, or tell me to stay in my seat. It's their job to follow directions from the pilots and flight attendants.

Parents are important. They follow directions from the crew. This helps the pilot and flight attendants make sure that everyone has a safe and comfortable flight. ■

Children Are Important Passengers

Children often help everyone on a plane have a safe and pleasant flight. Listening to parents and trying to follow directions is one way that children can help.

I will try to help mom and dad when we fly. They can tell me about the rules for flying. I will try to listen and follow those rules. My mom, dad, and everyone around us in the airplane will be pleased if I follow the airplane rules.

Pilots first—and moms and dads second—decide when it's okay for people to take off their seatbelt or move around.

Pilots decide when people can leave their seats. In every airplane there's a little picture of a seatbelt. It's also a light. When I am in the airplane, my mom or dad can show me where it is. There's a little seatbelt sign in each row.

The pilot turns the seatbelt sign on and off. If the seatbelt picture is on, that means everyone must keep their seatbelts on. It's the law.

I will try to listen to my parents and follow directions. This will help everyone to have a safe and comfortable flight. ▪

The New Social Story™ Book, 15th Anniversary Edition
© by Carol Gray, Future Horizons, Inc.

Is This Flight on Time?

Most flights are on time. Some flights are delayed. Other flights are cancelled. This happens with air travel.

Most flights are *on time*. *On time* means that everything is safe for the plane to fly at the scheduled time.

Sometimes, a flight is *delayed*. This means that there's a new, later time to take off, and a new, later time to land. This is okay. Sometimes it takes longer to make sure a plane is ready to fly.

Other times, a flight is *cancelled*. This means that the plane will not be taking off as planned. When this happens, passengers often fly on another plane.

Most planes fly on time. Some flights are delayed. Other flights are cancelled. This happens with air travel. That's Life on Planet Earth. ■

Why Are Some Flights Delayed?

A plane may be delayed at any time during a flight. A plane may be delayed before the passengers get on it. A plane may be delayed after the passengers are on it. Sometimes, a plane is delayed while it is in the air. Other times, a plane is delayed after it has landed. There are times when a plane is delayed more than once during a flight.

There are many reasons why a flight may be delayed. Something may need to be fixed. There may be a storm. The crew may need to rest. There may be a line of planes on the ground waiting to take off, or a line of planes in the sky waiting to land. There are other reasons a plane may be delayed, too.

At first, many passengers feel a little disappointed or frustrated when a flight is delayed. These negative feelings don't last for long, though. Passengers know that a delayed flight almost always means that care is being taken to keep everyone on the plane safe. Knowing that helps passengers feel patient, calm, and comfortable once again.

A flight may be delayed. There are many reasons why. Delaying a flight often helps to keep it safe. ■

The New Social Story™ Book, 15th Anniversary Edition
© by Carol Gray, Future Horizons, Inc.

A Wildfire Is near Our Home

There is a wildfire getting closer to our home. This makes this story very important.

Fire is the flame, heat, and light that is caused by burning. Fire can be helpful. Fire can also be a very serious problem. Fire is always dangerous. Knowing about fire helps people stay safe.

Fire can be helpful. People often use fire for heat and energy to keep their homes warm and comfortable, or to cook food. When camping, adults may build a campfire, or use fire to light a lantern. There are many ways that fire is helpful.

Adults know about the dangers of fire, and how to use fire safely. They know and follow all of the rules for using fire intelligently. They know, too, that it is very, very, very important to be careful with fire. That way fire stays safe, helpful, and under control.

Sometimes fire becomes a very big and serious problem. The fire spreads and gets larger. The people try to keep it under their control but the fire spreads too quickly. The fire becomes too big for them to put out. When this happens, people call the fire department.

When a fire is outside and spreading very quickly it is called a wildfire. Wildfires are a very, very, very, big and serious problem. They get bigger very fast. A wildfire is very, very, very, very difficult for people to control. Many times firefighters ask other firefighters to help get a wildfire back under control.

There is a wildfire about ___ miles away. It's difficult for the firemen to get it under control. To keep my family safe and healthy, we may be asked to leave our house. The firemen are watching the fire very closely. They will tell my mom or dad if it's important for us to leave our house. ▪

The New Social Story™ Book, 15th Anniversary Edition
© by Carol Gray, Future Horizons, Inc.

What Does *Evacuate* Mean?

Sometimes people are told to *evacuate* their house. *Evacuate* means *to empty and leave.* Sometimes, though, *evacuate* means *to take what is most important and leave the rest.*

Usually, a family is asked to evacuate because their house may be in danger. Fire is dangerous to a house. The house may burn. It's very important to keep the family safe and away from the fire. For this reason families are asked to evacuate their house. They are asked to go to a safer place.

Most families never have to evacuate their house. Once in a very long while, though, some families do have to evacuate. When people are told to evacuate a house, it is very, very, very important to follow that direction.

Evacuation is one way that parents keep their children safe. I may be able to help if my family has to evacuate our house. I may be able to help to keep the people in my family safe. Mom or Dad will have ideas about how I may help. ◼

Why Do We Have to Go?

Many children have questions about evacuation. Often they want to know why their family has to evacuate the house. Sometimes children will ask their mom or dad, "Why do we have to go?"

When firefighters tell a family to evacuate, it's very, very, very important for people to leave their house. Firefighters have studied fires for a long time. They are fire experts. Firefighters decide when a fire is too close and people have to evacuate their houses. It's intelligent to listen and follow their directions.

Sometimes, it may seem that a fire is not that close. It may seem like it would be okay to stay. The problem is, when a fire is out of control it spreads quickly. That is why firefighters ask families to evacuate when it is still safe to go, before the fire is very close.

Firefighters decide when a fire is too close. They tell people when it is time to evacuate. If a firefighter says, "It's time to evacuate," it's time to evacuate. Following the directions of firefighters helps people stay safe. ■

The New Social Story™ Book, 15th Anniversary Edition
© by Carol Gray, Future Horizons, Inc.

People Would Rather Stay in their Houses

People evacuate a house because they have to leave. If they had a choice, they would choose to stay and do what they usually do. They wish the fire was out. They wish their home was farther away from the fire. They wish the fire was under control. Wishing doesn't put a fire out, though. If it did, the fire would be out by now.

By the time people grow to become adults, they have learned to do things they don't want to do without whining or having a tantrum. They may feel sad, nervous, or uncomfortable, but they know it's important to keep thinking and working to keep their family safe.

Sometimes adults help themselves feel better by remembering that life isn't always like this. They know that fires end and someday it will be possible to do the things that they usually do. That's when adults say things like, "It will be nice when life gets back to normal." That helps them to remember life without wildfires, and they feel better.

If my mom and dad say, "It's time to evacuate," it's important to follow their direction. ■

Maybe I Could Do That

Someday, I will be an adult. What will I do? It may be fun to think about that.

There are people who work to save Planet Earth's resources. Maybe I could do that.

There are people who sell tickets at the movie theatre. Maybe I could do that.

There are people who write poems and sonnets. Maybe I could do that.

There are people who work at the radio station. Maybe I could do that.

There are people who teach. Maybe I could do that.

There are people who stock the shelves at the grocery store. Maybe I could do that.

The New Social Story™ Book, 15th Anniversary Edition
© by Carol Gray, Future Horizons, Inc.

There are people who find cures for diseases. Maybe I could do that.

There are people who design and draw. Maybe I could do that.

There are people who work in big cities. Maybe I could do that.

There are people who work outdoors. Maybe I could do that.

Someday, I will be an adult. What will I do? Just watch as I answer that. ■

CHAPTER 15

Social Articles

Social Stories are provided in a highly structured but also flexible writing format. They are right at home, describing how toilets work to a toddler, and are equally capable of describing the ins and outs of making an effective apology to an adult. As Social Stories keep pace with their growing Audience, the topics, format, font, and vocabulary change as well. By the time a child reaches adolescence, the tried-and-true Social Stories yield to their more advanced form, *Social Articles*. My name is Carol Gray, creator of these articles, and it's my pleasure to introduce you to this rarely used yet valuable literary format.

Social Articles meet all the same criteria as Social Stories, with several characteristics that distinguish them from their Story-based counterparts. Social Articles use a format that incorporates Times New Roman font, columns, and advanced vocabulary. They are never written in the Audience voice, and rarely contain any first-person statements. Charts and figures are frequently used to organize or highlight ideas and may replace more traditional or elementary illustrations.

Dr. Tony Attwood and I wrote the first Social Article, *Gray's Guide to Compliments*. We surveyed workshop audiences to gather much of the information, asking questions like, "How frequently do you compliment your spouse?" That information was subsequently summarized in a 22-page workbook for adults with autism.

> ### Figure 1: Frequent characteristics of a Social Article
>
> - Address abstract or more advanced concepts
> - Times New Roman font
> - Columns
> - Advanced vocabulary
> - Never written in the Audience voice, and often do not contain first-person statements
> - Charts and figures to enhance or highlight information

Social Articles have a range of difficulty that is similar to that of Social Stories. I consider one of the Social Articles in this chapter, *Why People Take Baths or Showers*, as the most elementary version of a Social Article. It lies right on the seamless border between Social Stories and Articles. The remaining articles in this chapter appear in order of difficulty, each demonstrating several of the characteristics described previously and listed in Figure 1 (above).

One final note: As I mentioned, Social Articles are never written in the Audience voice and thus, first-person statements are often not included. However, the *Author* may serve as the voice of an article. In this case, the author introduces himself or herself and his or her background, with care to identify any personal opinions or bias as information is shared. This makes it possible to provide general insights and conclusions about social concepts and skills or to express opinions or share advice through an opportunity that would not be available otherwise. This is demonstrated in *Apologizing for an Unintentional Mistake*, which closes this chapter and volume. I hope you enjoy it.

I wish you all the best as you develop Social Articles and, of course, Social Stories.

The New Social Story™ Book, 15th Anniversary Edition
© by Carol Gray, Future Horizons, Inc.

Why People Take Baths or Showers

People take baths and showers. They have been taking baths since 3,300 B.C. During the Roman Empire, people began bathing as a daily ritual. Understanding why people take baths and showers may make it easier for me to take my bath/shower.

History is full of stories about bathtubs and bathing. The ancient Greek inventor, Archimedes, noticed that when he got into his tub, the level of the water would rise. He began using tubs to measure how big items were by noticing the amount of water they displaced in his tub. This may be an interesting story, but it is also a unique reason to use a bathtub. Throughout history, people have taken baths or showers to get clean. But why do they do this?

People take baths to get clean or to feel or smell better. Being clean, washing away dirt and germs, is a healthy habit. For many people, being dirty is a little uncomfortable and even a little itchy. Sometimes dirty people smell bad. A bath or a shower makes their skin feel comfortable again, and makes them smell better, too.

People also take baths because of other people. They are concerned about what other people may think. Since so many people think being clean is comfortable, just being around someone who is dirty or smelly can make them uncomfortable. Many people don't want to be around a dirty person for long. They may also not want to be friends with someone who is often dirty or smells bad. So people sometimes take a bath or shower so that others will feel comfortable.

People have been taking baths throughout history. I am a part of history. By taking a bath or a shower, I may be more comfortable—and others will be more comfortable—as I make my mark on history. ■

Sharing Planet Earth

People live on Planet Earth. They share it. Sometimes they share it well, but other times it's harder for people to share Planet Earth.

People on Planet Earth share some things easily. Day and night are one example. When one side of the planet has day, the other has night. There are times when some people on the planet get a lot of daylight, and others get a lot less. But even though daylight and night are unequal, people seem to be okay with that. The seasons are another example. When one part of the planet has summer, somewhere else it is fall. Many people love summer, and there are parts of Planet Earth that get a lot more of it than others. People seem to be okay with that, too.

Even though the sun and seasons are really big and important, people share them easily, without having to think much about it. Sometimes parents may tell their children that they "need to learn how to share." Children share sun and seasons as easily as their parents. Here's a theory: It's easier for people to share what they can't possibly own or to share when it is just a part of their routine.

People on Planet Earth have to think and work together to share other things. This includes adults. The list of things that are harder to share is a lot longer than this whole book. Here are six of them: money, malted milk balls, oil, televisions, macaroni and cheese, and neighborhoods. The things on this list are smaller than the sun and may be less important than a season, but they are hard for many people to share.

Here's another theory: It's more difficult for people to share something that has a limited supply. Sometimes even adults have to think about how to share things like that. They try to teach their children to share, too.

People live on Planet Earth. They need to share it. Sometimes they share it easily, but other times they have to think about it. Sharing is a part of life for the adults and children of Planet Earth. ■

The New Social Story™ Book, 15th Anniversary Edition
© by Carol Gray, Future Horizons, Inc.

The Evening News: How We Changed Today

At the same time every day, the evening news is shown on television. It starts at the same time each day, usually with the same person, called the anchor, who reports the news.

Some anchors have a phrase that they use somewhere in the opening of the evening news, like "Nightly news begins now." They use it with each newscast. They often have another phrase they use each day to end the news, like, "And that's the way it is."

To watch the evening news, many people sit in the same chair, at about the same time each day, to watch the news. They watch the same station. Same time. Same channel. Same anchor. Same phrases. Same chair.

The news itself, though, is never, ever the same as the day before. The news reports change.

Expected changes are usually not newsworthy. They are not big news. What would those reports sound like? "It's Fall here in Vermont. I'm standing in front of a tree. It was here yesterday. It dropped a few leaves today, though."

The most newsworthy changes are often those that are unwelcome and unexpected. The very biggest, most important changes make the evening news everywhere.

Here's a theory: The evening news reports change. How news is reported, though, stays pretty much the same. For people on Planet Earth, learning about change seems to work best if it is done the same way each day. ■

At the End of Each Day: A Little Bit Changed and Mostly the Same

Here's a theory: At the end of each day, Planet Earth is a little bit changed and mostly the same.

A lot changes in a day. Each day:

- 216,000 babies are born. They are Planet Earth's newest people, until tomorrow.
- Every person is a day older than the day before.
- Every building, car, sofa, television, and many, many other things become a day older.
- Many people change their location. Some peo-ple drive their car, take a bus, ride a train, or take a boat to another place. They may fly to another place, too. About 49,000 airline flights are made each day.
- Some plants get bigger, all plants get older, some trees fall.
- About 2,600 earthquakes happen, most of them very small and unnoticed.

At the end of each day, it is likely that there have been more changes on Planet Earth than anyone could count before the next day.

For all the changes that happen each day, from space, Planet Earth always looks pretty much the same. The really, really big things don't change a lot. The Earth trav-els around the sun the same. The Earth turns the same way. Oceans, mountains, riv-ers, and valleys are in about the same place that they have been in for many, many years. People don't need to make a new topographical map of Earth each day!

People depend on Planet Earth to stay mostly the same. It helps them to plan their year, month, and day. It helps them to know pretty much what life will be like tomorrow. It helps them to feel comfortable here and focus on what is important to them.

At the end of each day, with all of the changes on Planet Earth, it's still pretty much the same. It's a reality that helps many people fall asleep each night. ■

The New Social Story™ Book, 15th Anniversary Edition
© by Carol Gray, Future Horizons, Inc.

Apologizing for an Unintentional Mistake

Please note: In this article, the pronoun 'he' is used in reference to an individual, whether male or female, in place of the more awkward "he and/or she."

My name is Carol Gray. I am not an expert on apologies, although admittedly I do at times make mistakes that require them. This gives me a wealth of experience that, along with my observations of others over the last several decades, provides an extensive apologetic background. This article presents my theories and thoughts about apologies and the seven characteristics of those that are most likely to be the most effective.

My general thoughts and theories may not be true in every culture or situation.

It's important to keep in mind that there are almost always exceptions when people are involved. Regardless, I will try to the best of my ability to describe accurately what I have found to be true about effective apologies *most of the time.*

According to dictionary. reference.com, the most common meaning of *apology* is "... a written or spoken expression of one's regret, remorse, or sorrow for having insulted, failed, injured, or wronged another." I also found three others, but in this article, I am focusing on the meaning that I have quoted here.

People make mistakes with one another. It's inevitable. No human inhabitant of Planet Earth has a mistake score of zero. Some errors are intentional, and others are unintentional.

When I was three years old, I placed my sister's doll suitcase in the toilet. My intent was to put it in the toilet, and I did. It was a bad idea that became an intentional mistake, and it made a perfectly good doll suitcase very soggy. My sister was upset.

I estimate that I have made many more *unintentional* mistakes. These are the mistakes where *I meant* no harm, I wasn't *thinking* about hurting anyone, but I *did* harm. For example, I have said things without thinking it through and ended up causing someone to feel unhappy or angry. I've also accidently damaged something that does not belong to me. I've also inconvenienced people without knowing it until it was too late and the damage was already done. In the remainder of this discussion I'm going to focus on those unintentional errors that negatively impact others and the apologies most likely to be effective.

Many people feel anxious or uneasy when they realize they've made a mistake and need to apologize. Understanding where the discomfort is coming from may help. Apologizing may be uncomfortable because:

1. There was no negative intent, so realizing that someone was hurt is an unpleasant surprise or a shock;

2. It may be difficult to take responsibility for a mistake when it was accidental; or

3. The person hurt or inconvenienced by the mistake often feels sad or angry, and thus is likely to be not as much fun to approach or chat with as when he is calm and happy.

This is not a complete list. There are other reasons why apologizing for an unintentional mistake may be uncomfortable.

Apologizing is not *always* uncomfortable. A lot depends on the people involved and the severity of the mistake. One thing is for sure—everyone makes unintentional mistakes, and an apology is often a helpful antidote.

Before going any further, it's important to note that apologies can take many forms. There are verbal apologies, emailed apologies, apologies attached to a small gift or flowers, or apologies written on the inside of a greeting card. Sometimes a person may make something like a cake, cookies, picture, or something else to include as part of an apology.

Once a person decides to apologize, there are seven things that he or she can do (Figure 1) to increase the odds that it will improve the feelings of everyone involved.

1. The best apologies are sincere. The person who is apologizing regrets that his words or actions have hurt or inconvenienced the other person.

Figure 1: Seven characteristics of an apology most likely to be effective following an unintentional mistake.

The best apologies:
1. Are sincere.
2. Use good timing.
3. Begin with a name.
4. Describe the mistake.
5. Express regret.
6. Acknowledge the other person's feelings.
7. Are responsible.

2. The best apologies use good timing. First, apologizing sooner is much better than apologizing later, and apologizing later is better than apologizing a lot later. The less time that passes between a mistake and its apology, the better. Second, People learn to deliver an apology when the other person has time to talk and listen. It's risky to apologize to a person who is currently busy, distracted, or stressed by another situation. For example, a boy who tries to apologize to his mom while she is rushing to prepare a dinner party for eight eminent guests is using poor timing. Unless, that is, the boy is sorry that his frog just jumped into the filled punch bowl. In this case, it's not good news, not a good time, but Mom needs to know he is sorry now.

3. The best apologies begin with a name. For many people, hearing their name recruits their attention. It personalizes an

apology right from the start. Waiting for an acknowledgment, for eyes to look up from a current activity or another indication of attention is a good idea. In addition to someone's name, many people find that saying something like, "I need to talk to you. Is this a good time?" is a great way to determine if the timing is right (described in #2) before continuing by listening for the answer.

4. The best apologies describe the mistake. In my experience, there have been times when I start to apologize, and then realize the other person doesn't quite know what I am talking about. Life gets busy, many things happen, and it may take a person a while to focus on a specific event in the past, even if it is the immediate past. For this reason, the best apologies include a description of the mistake, even if the other person was there at the time. Including a description of the mistake is absolutely critical if the other person is not aware that a mistake has been made. For example, "Remember when you loaned me your jacket yesterday? I wore it to the game, and as I took it off it fell into the mud and water."

5. The best apologies express regret and mean it. I have a theory about the phrase, "I am sorry." It's difficult for many people to say this phrase,

because doing so feels like an admission of guilt. When a mistake is unintentional, admitting guilt often doesn't quite seem to fit the situation. "I'm sorry" doesn't always mean a person is guilty. The details surrounding the mistake do that. It often simply is an expression of regret that means *I am sorry this happened.*

6. The best apologies include an acknowledgment of the *other person's* feelings. For the boy with the frog in mom's punch bowl, saying *"Mom, I know you want things right for the party,"* supports Mom and may turn efforts toward a solution sooner. Or, in the case of the muddy jacket, a statement like *"I know this is your favorite jacket,"* may dissolve understandable disappointment or anger.

7. The best apologies are responsible. They include an offer to help solve the problem, a promise to do things differently in the future, or both.

Continuing with our examples, the boy may return the frog to his cage, offer to help clean the bowl and make a new batch of punch, as well as promise to keep the frog away from future dinner parties. In terms of the jacket, including an offer to clean it is an important part of the apology. Adding evidence of thoughts regarding next time, as in, "I wish I had been more careful and put the jacket in my backpack" begins to rebuild trust.

I've listed these characteristics as a guide and a summary of my own experiences and observations of others. They are definitely not intended as a series of defined steps.

An apology may be effective without meeting all seven characteristics. That's definitely why I mentioned earlier that, whenever people are involved, there is an exception to every rule! ∎

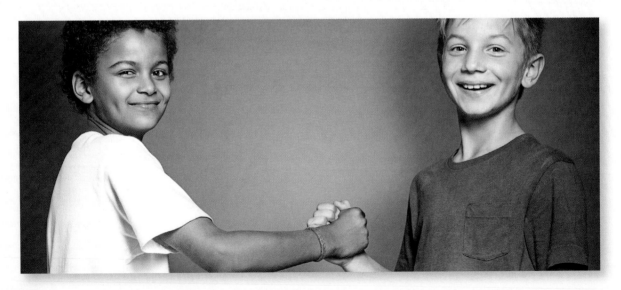

Glossary

What is a Glossary?

A *dictionary* is an alphabetical list of words and definitions. People use a dictionary to learn how to spell or say a word, or to find out what a word means.

A *glossary* is an alphabetical list of words, too. It describes the meanings of difficult words or phrases in a book. This is the glossary for *The New Social Story Book*.

Each word has meaning. Some words, like *dictionary* and *glossary*, each have one meaning. Many other words have more than one meaning. The word *word* is one of them. *Word* may mean *a spoken sound or set of sounds that has meaning*, *a piece of news*, *a short speech*, or *a promise*.

Once in a while, people need a dictionary or glossary to help them with words. They may need help with words like *transform*, which is listed in this glossary. This is to be expected. *Expect* is another one of the words in this glossary. This glossary has many other words and phrases in it, too.

There is a special section at the end titled Words and Phrases that Describe Frequency. It has many words and phrases that people use to describe how often something happens or occurs. In that section are words like *sometimes* and *never*, as well as phrases like *now and then*, or *most of the time*. These, and other words and phrases like them, are used frequently in this book. (Even the word *frequently* is in that section). Because the meanings for many of these words and phrases are so close, they are described as a group.

In this glossary, each word or phrase is listed in boldface. It is followed by the part of speech in parentheses, like this: ( ). A definition is next, followed by the word used in a sample sentence. Sample sentences are from this book, and appear in italics. For example, the word *glossary* would appear like this:

Glossary (noun)
A *glossary* is an alphabetical list of difficult or unusual words and phrases found in a book.
    Sample sentence: *This glossary has many other words and phrases in it, too.*

People may use the following glossary to look up the meanings of some of the more difficult words and phrases in this book. ■

The New Social Story™ Book, 15th Anniversary Edition
© by Carol Gray, Future Horizons, Inc.

Glossary

Calm (adjective)
Calm means quiet, peaceful, relaxed; not upset.
> Sample sentence: *It's important to try to stay calm.*

Calm voice (adjective+noun)
A *calm voice* is peaceful and friendly, comfortable for other people to listen to.
> Sample sentence: *When I am happy, it may be easy for me to talk with my calm voice and cooperative words.*

Cooperate (verb)
Cooperate means to work or play together in a helpful way, for the same goal.
> Sample sentence: *When people want help, they cooperate with you.*

Cooperation (noun)
Cooperation is the act of working or playing together in a helpful way, for the same goal.
> Sample sentence: *Cooperation is a clue that my sister wants my help.*

Cooperative (adjective)
Cooperative means willing to help or cooperate with others (*see* Cooperate).
> Sample sentence: *When a fun activity ends, I will try to stay calm and cooperative.*

Cooperative words (adjective+noun)

Cooperative words are single words, phrases, or sentences that help people work and play together for the same goal. Cooperative words are stated in a calm and friendly tone of voice (*see* Calm voice).

> Sample sentence: *Talking with respect is using a calm, controlled voice with cooperative words.*

Expect (verb)

When *expect* is used in this book, it has one of two meanings.
Expect may mean to think ahead, to guess that something will probably happen.

> Sample sentence: *As an inventor, he expected to make mistakes.*

2. *Expect* may mean to believe that something should happen.

> Sample sentence: *Once in a while, though, children are expected to shake hands.*

Experience (noun)

When *experience* is used in this book, it has one of two meanings.

Experience may mean an event or activity, something that a person sees, hears, or does.

> Sample sentence: *A true story often describes an experience.*

Experience may mean knowledge that is gained by doing something, or by practicing a skill.

> Sample sentence: *They have a lot of experience.*

Frustrate/Frustrating (verb)

Frustrate means to be stopped or kept from reaching a goal, or unable to do what a person wants to do.

> Sample sentence: *Waiting to open a gift may be a little frustrating, especially for children.*

The New Social Story™ Book, 15th Anniversary Edition
© by Carol Gray, Future Horizons, Inc.

Guess (verb or noun)

When *guess* is used in this book, it has one of two meanings.

Guess may mean to believe something *may* be true, correct, or the right thing to do, without enough information to know for sure if it is true, correct, or the right thing to do. (verb)

> Sample sentence: *Another way that adults often say yes is, "Okay, I guess," or back- wards, "I guess it's okay."*

Guess may mean a belief without enough information to know for sure if it is correct or true. (noun)

> Sample sentence: *Grandpa says that many people like to wrap gifts, so his guess is that they will wrap them this year, too.*

Predict (verb)

To *predict* is to know something will happen ahead of time; often it is a guess that is based on information. Weather forecasters try to predict the weather.

> Sample sentences: *No one can predict exactly when someone may try to bully another person. No one can predict exactly what a student may do in a bullying attempt.*

Step (noun)

When *step* is used in this book, it has one of three meanings.

Step may mean putting one foot forward, backward, or sideways.

> Sample sentence: *I had to keep repeating "excuse me" every few steps.*

Step may mean a place to put one's foot to move up or down. One step is one part of a set of stairs or staircase.

> Sample sentence: *For example, they may forget their lunch, trip going up steps, or dial a phone number incorrectly.*

Step may also mean one of a series of actions that complete a task, or reach a goal.

>Sample sentence: *We will complete it step by step, following the directions and answering the questions together.*

Social Story (noun)

A *Social Story* is a true story that describes a situation, skill, or idea. It is researched, written, and illustrated according to ten criteria or characteristics.

>Sample sentence: The New Social Story™ Book *by Carol Gray contains many Social Stories.*

Surprise (verb or noun)

When *surprise* is used in this book, it has one of two meanings.

Surprise may mean something that happens unexpectedly. (verb)

>Sample sentence: *Children may be surprised to learn that most adults like to say "yes" whenever they can.*

Surprise may mean something that is not expected, for example, a statement, gift, action, or event. (noun)

>Sample sentence: *Many people think that nice surprises are fun.*

Theory (noun)

A *theory* is a guess or opinion that explains how or why something happens. A theory is often based on some facts, or experience, but not proven.

>Sample sentence: *Here's a theory: It's easier for people to share what they can't possibly own, or to share when it is just a part of their routine.*

Thing (noun)

In this book, *thing* has one of seven meanings.

Thing(s) may mean any real object(s) or item(s).

> Sample sentence: *He invented many other things, too.*

Thing(s) may mean almost any topic(s) or idea.

> Sample sentence: *When I look at these photos, it reminds me of one thing that I have learned about parties.*

Thing(s) may mean almost any activity (activities).

> Sample sentence: *There are things that I like to do.*

Thing(s) may mean one person's clothing, toys, or personal items.

> Sample sentence: *We'll put most of my toys and other things in moving boxes.*

Thing(s) may mean almost any statement(s) that is said, or written.

> Sample sentence: *We try to say the same thing, but with respect.*

Thing(s) may mean almost any event(s).

> Sample sentence: *Sometimes things happen, though, and people cannot come.*

Thing(s) may mean the condition of a friendship, relationship, event, or activity.

> Sample sentence: *Soon, they want to make things right again.*

There are more meanings for the word *thing* in the dictionary. In this book, when *thing* is used in a sentence, it has one of these listed meanings.

That's Life on Planet Earth (phrase)

That's Life of Planet Earth is a phrase that usually follows a description of an experience that almost all people have in common. These may be comfortable, good, experiences. Or, they may be uncomfortable or unwanted experiences. Either way, they are a part of life for almost all people on Planet Earth.

Sample uses of the phrase, *That's Life on Planet Earth:*

Sad is an uncomfortable feeling. It's okay for people to feel sad. When people feel sad they try to find a way to be happy again. That's Life on Planet Earth.

Mistakes are a part of Life on Planet Earth. That is correct.

Permission is needed when a child has an idea, and it's an adult's decision to make. Sometimes children get the permission that they need, other times they don't. Either way, that's Life on Planet Earth!

This is Okay (phrase)

This is okay is a phrase that usually follows a description of a surprising, unwanted or uncomfortable situation. *This is okay* means that even though a situation may not be what someone would like, it needs to happen—or will happen—in the way just described. *This is okay* also means that while a situation may be surprising, unwanted, or uncomfortable, it is safe.

Sample uses of the phrase, *This is okay:*

The truth is, adults don't know everything. This is okay.

The line of people, with me in it, may need to stop and wait now and then. This is okay.

Sometimes, I may go to the babysitter's house to stay until Mom or Dad come back for me. This is okay.

Transform (verb)

Transform means to completely change how a living being or thing looks or functions (how it works).

Sample sentence: *Just watch me transform as I grow!*

Transformation (noun)
A *transformation* is a big change in how a living being or thing looks or functions (how it works).

Sample sentence: *This is the transformation stage.*

Transformer (noun)
In the dictionary, a *transformer* is a device that changes electrical voltage. In this book, *transformer* is a living being that makes big changes in appearance or function (how it works).

Sample sentence: *A butterfly is a real transformer.*

Welcome (verb, noun, or adjective)
When *welcome* is used in this book, it has one of two meanings.

Welcome may mean to give someone a friendly greeting as they arrive (verb).

Sample sentence: *Welcome to Fort Able!*

Welcome may mean to receive in a friendly way (adjective).

Sample sentence: *Here's a theory: Expected and welcome changes are the easiest.*

Unexpected (adjective)
Unexpected means happening as a surprise, without any warning.

Sample sentence: *Since fires and tornadoes are often unexpected, it's important to practice for them that way.*

Unwelcome (adjective)
Unwelcome means not wanted, accepted, or welcome.

Sample sentence: *A flat tire on a car is an unexpected and unwelcome surprise.*

WORDS AND PHRASES ABOUT FREQUENCY

Many words and phrases describe how often something happens, or its *frequency*. For example, the word "always" means continuously, every time, or on every occasion. The word "never" means at no time, not on any occasion. "Always" and "never" have opposite meanings: "always" is every time, "never" is not ever.

In the drawing below, "always" and "never" are placed at opposite ends of the line to show the opposite meanings. Several people were asked to arrange words and phrases from this book, according to their frequency. The results are placed on the line between "never" and "always." The closer the word or phrase is to "always," the greater its frequency. Words with similar meanings are the same color. To figure out the meaning of a word or phrase, look at its color and placement on the line. There are many other words and phrases used to describe how often something happens, but these are the words and phrases used in this book. ■

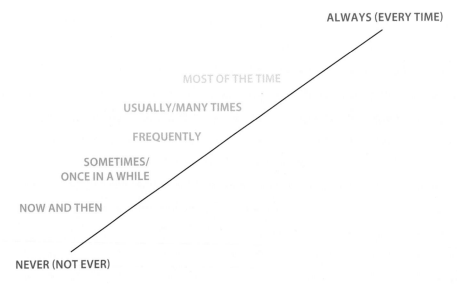

ALWAYS (EVERY TIME)

MOST OF THE TIME

USUALLY/MANY TIMES

FREQUENTLY

SOMETIMES/
ONCE IN A WHILE

NOW AND THEN

NEVER (NOT EVER)

Foreword to the 10th Anniversary Edition

Carol Gray originally developed Social Stories™ in 1991 from working directly and collaboratively with children with autism and Asperger's Syndrome. For nearly twenty years, she has been modifying the guidelines for writing Social Stories™, based on extensive personal experience and feedback from parents, teachers, and the children themselves. The ideas and strategies have matured over the years and Social Stories™ have now been examined independently in numerous research studies published in scientific journals. There is no doubt that the use of Social Stories™ in education and therapy is what scientists describe as "evidence-based practice." Social Stories™ really do work.

Whenever I learn that Carol Gray is working on a new publication, I become quite excited in anticipation of reading her latest insights into how children with an autism spectrum disorders perceive and experience the world. I know that her innovative ideas and strategies will be incorporated into my clinical practice, and that I will be recommending the latest publication to teachers, parents, and colleagues. As I read the manuscript for the *The New Social Story Book*, I thought, "Carol, you have done it again!" She has written another exceptional resource that will improve not only social understanding but also self-understanding. Carol has remarkable insight into the world of autism and the neurotypical world, and her Social Stories™ are for members of both—improving mutual understanding, communication, and acceptance.

This book is complementary to Carol's other publications and provides examples of Social Stories™ that can be used without modification, or adapted and edited to suit a specific child and his or her unique abilities and circumstances. I recommend *The New Social Story Book* for those who are new to the area of autism and Asperger's Syndrome as a parent, teacher, therapist, or psychologist, and also for those with considerable experience writing Social Stories™. I often refer to my copy as a source of guidance and inspiration when I am working with a child who has Asperger's Syndrome.

From her extensive experience of working with children, parents, and teachers, Carol knows the problem areas—the "hot topics." These include coping with change, making mistakes, specific situations (such as attending a birthday party or being an airline passenger), and managing and expressing emotions. Carol chooses her words very carefully. Great thought, wisdom, and talent went into this new publication. There are some parts I will always remember, in particular the statement, "Adults are children who kept getting older," and the Social Story™ for when "some gifts are disappointing." I know that children with an autism spectrum disorder and neurotypical adults alike will enjoy and appreciate the comprehensive explanations and the sage advice in *The New Social Story Book*.

TONY ATTWOOD, PH.D.

References

References for Stories in The New Social Story™ Book

(listed by title in sequential order)

The Transformers Around Us: Butterflies
Montana State University. Butterflies: The children's butterfly site. Life cycle of butterflies and moths. Retrieved October 4, 2009 from *www.kidsbutterfly.org/life-cycle*

The Transformers Around Us: Frogs.
All About Frogs.org. Life cycle of a frog. Retrieved October 4, 2009 from *http://allaboutfrogs. org/weird/general/cycle.html*

The Transformers Around Us: Ladybugs
Mrs. Seagraves QUEST class homepage. The life cycle of the ladybug. Retrieved October 4, 2009 from *www.geocities.com/sseagraves/ladybuglifecycle.htm*

Thomas Edison and Mistakes
Google. Cynthia-ga. Did Thomas Edison really say this? Retrieved on October 1, 2009 from *http://answers.google.com/answers/threadview/id/747226.html*

Why Do People Shake Hands?
Ramsey, L. Shaking Hands Throughout History and Around the World. Retrieved August 8, 2009 at *www.mannersthatsell.com/articles/shakinghands.html*

Bullying: What to Think, Say, and Do (Chapter 7)
Gray, C. (2004). Gray's guide to bullying: The original series of articles parts I-III. Enclosed student workbook: How to respond to a bullying attempt: What to think, say, and do (1-8). Jenison Autism Journal, 16:1.

Moving To a New Community

All listed online resources retrieved on September 12, 2009.
City of Shelton, Connecticut. *www.cityofshelton.org/*
LaFayette Public School. *www.trulia.com/schools/CT-Shelton/Lafayette_Elementary_School/*
Rich and Ben's Hair Styling. *http://yellowpages.lycos.com/search?C=Barbers&L=Shelton%2C+Connecticut&diktf-c=5D914DF6529AF950D797FDEF3EF5F419B795CAEE7864*
Beechwood Supermarket. *www.beechwoodmarket.com*
City of Garretson, South Dakota. *www.garretsonsd.com/index.php?option=com_content&view=article&id=42&Itemid=17*
Garretson Elementary School. *http://garretson.k12.sd.us/*
Brandon Plaza Barbers. *http://yp.yahoo.com/yp/Garretson_SD/Personal_Care_Barbers/8109930.html*
Garretson Food Center. *www.garretsonsd.com* .

Washing My Hands

Mayo Clinic. Hand washing: Do's and don'ts. Retrieved September 19, 2009 from *www.mayoclinic.com/health/hand-washing/HQ00407*

Why People Take Baths or Showers

All listed online resources retrieved on August 15, 2009. Radmore, C. The evolution of bathing and showers. *www.talewins.com/family/historyofshowers.htm* Wikipedia. Archimedes. *http://en.wikipedia.org/wiki/Archimedes*

It's My Teacher's Decision

Gray, C. (Author) & Shelley, M. (Director/Producer). (2006). It's the teacher's decision (motion picture). In Storymovies™: Social concepts and skills at school. United States: The Specialminds Foundation.

Talking to a Teacher with Respect

Gray, C. (Author) & Shelley, M. (Director/Producer). (2006). Talking to a teacher with respect. (motion picture). In Storymovies™: Social concepts and skills at school. United States: The Specialminds Foundation.

What Is Practice?

Gray, C. (Author) & Shelley, M. (Director/Producer). (2006). What is practice? (motion picture). In Storymovies™: Social concepts and skills at school. United States: The Specialminds Foundation.

Mistakes Happen on the Way to Learning.

Gray, C. (Author) & Shelley, M. (Director/Producer). (2006). Mistakes may happen on the way to learning (motion picture). In Storymovies™: Social concepts and skills at school. United States: The Specialminds Foundation.

Good Questions for a Small Group Project.

Gray, C. (Author) & Shelley, M. (Director/Producer). (2006). What is a good question? (motion picture). In Storymovies™: Social concepts and skills at school. United States: The Specialminds Foundation.

At the End of Each Day: A Little Bit Changed and Mostly the Same.

All listed online resources retrieved on October 1, 2009. Answers.com: WikiAnswers. How many babies are born each day in the world? *http://wiki.answers.com/Q/How_many_babies_are_born_every_day_in_the_world* Answerbag. com. How many commercial airline flights are there per day in the world? *www.answerbag. com/q_view/93860*

Answerbag.com. How many earthquakes happen each day? *www.answerbag.com/q_view/93860*

References for The New Social Story™ Book Glossary

Agnes, M. (Ed.). (1999). Webster's new world children's dictionary (2nd Edition). Cleveland, Ohio: Wiley Publishing, Inc.

Agnes, M. (Ed). (2003). Webster's new world dictionary (4th Edition). New York, N.Y: Pocket Books, Simon & Schuster, Inc.

Delahunty, A. (2002). Barron's first thesaurus. Hauppauge, N.Y: Barron's Educational Series, Inc.

Houghton Mifflin Harcourt. (2007). The American heritage student dictionary. Boston, MA: Houghton Mifflin Harcourt Publishing Company.

Leany, C. (2008). Junior dictionary & thesaurus. New York, N.Y: Barnes & Noble.

Levey, J.S. (Ed.). (1990). Macmillan first dictionary. New York, N.Y: Simon & Schuster Books for Young Readers.

Levey, J.S. (Ed.). (2006). First dictionary. New York, N.Y: Scholastic.

Morris, C.G. (Ed.) (2007). Macmillan fully illustrated dictionary for children. New York, N.Y: Simon & Schuster Books for Young Readers.

Scholastic, Inc. (2005). Scholastic pocket dictionary. U.S.A.: Scholastic, Inc.

Social Story™ Research and Related References

Agosta, E., Graetz, J. E., Mastropieri, M. A. & Scruggs, T. E. (2004). "Teacher-researcher partnerships to improve social behaviour though social stories." *Intervention in Schools and Clinic* 39 (5) 276 – 287.

Barry, L. M. & Burlew, S. B. (2004). "Using social stories to teach choice and play skills to children with autism." *Focus on Autism and Other Developmental Disabilities* 19 (1) 45-51.

Bledsoe, R., Smith, B. and Simpson, R. L. (2003). "Use of a social story intervention to improve mealtime skills of an adolescent with Asperger syndrome." *Autism* 7 (3) 289-295.

Brownell, M. (2002). "Musically adapted social stories to modify behaviors in students with autism: Four case studies." *Journal of Music Therapy* 39, 117-144.

Chalk M. (2003). Social stories for adults with autism and learning difficulties. *Good Autism Practice* 4(2), pp. 3-7.

Committee on Educational Interventions for Children with Autism. (2001). "Family roles." In C. Lord & J.P. McGee (Eds.), *Educating children with autism*. Washington, DC: National Academies Press.

Del Valle, P. R., McEachern, A. G. & Chambers, H. D. (2001). "Using social stories with autistic children." *Journal of Poetry Therapy* 14 (4) 187-197.

Erangey, K. (2001). "Using social stories as a parent of a child with an ASD." *Good Autism Practice* 2 (1) 309-323.

Gastgeb, H.Z., Strauss, M.S., & Minshew, N.J. (2006). "Do individuals with autism process categories differently? The effect of typicality and development." *Child Development* 77, 1717–1729.

Gray, C. (1998). "The advanced social story workbook." *The Morning News* 10(2), 1–21.

Gray, C. (2004). "Social stories 10.0: The new defining criteria and guidelines." *Jenison Autism Journal* 15, 2–21.

Gray, C.A. & Garand, J.D. (1993). "Social stories: Improving responses of students with autism with accurate social information." *Focus on Autistic Behavior* 8, 1–10.

Gray, C. (1998a). "Social stories and comic strip conversations with students with Asperger syndrome and high functioning autism." In: E. Schopler, G. Mesibov & L. Kunce (Eds.). *Asperger syndrome or high functioning autism?* (pp. 167-198). New York: Plenum Press.

Hagiwara, T., & Myles, B. S. (1999). "A multimedia social story intervention: Teaching skills to children with autism." *Focus on Autism and Other Developmental Disabilities* 14, 82-95.

Howley, M. (2001). "An investigation into the impact of social stories on the behaviour and social understanding of four pupils with autistic spectrum disorder." In R. Rose and Grosvenor (Eds) (2001). *Doing research in special education*. London: David Fulton.

Howley, M.,& Arnold,E. (2005). *Revealing the hidden social code*. London: Jessica Kingsley.

Ivey, M.L., Heflin, L.J., & Alberto, P. (2004). "The use of social stories to promote independent behaviors in novel events for children with PDD-NOS (autism spectrum disorder)." *Focus on Autism and Other Developmental Disabilities* 19, 164–176.

Jones, D., Swift, D., & Johnson, M. (1988). "Nondeliberate memory for a novel event among pre-schoolers." *Developmental Psychology* 24, 641-645.

Klinger, L.G., & Dawson, G. (2001). "Prototype formation in autism." *Development and Psychology* 13, 111–124.

Kluth, P., & Schwarz, P. (2008). *Just give him the whale! 20 ways to use fascinations, areas of expertise, and strengths to support students with autism*. Baltimore: Paul H. Brookes Publishing Co.

Kuoch, H., & Mirenda, P. (2003). "Social story interventions for young children with autism spectrum disorders." *Focus on Autism and Other Developmental Disorders* 18, 219–227.

Kuttler, S., Myles, B. S., & Carlson, J. K. (1998). "The use of social stories to reduce precursors to tantrum behaviour in a student with autism." *Focus on Autism and Other Developmental Disabilities* 12, 176-182.

Lorimer, P. A., Simpson, R., Myles, B. S. & Ganz, J. (2002). "The use of social stories as a preventative behavioral intervention in a home setting with a child with autism." *Journal of Positive Behavioral Interventions* 4 (1) 53-60.

Miller, D. (2002). *Reading with meaning: Teaching comprehension in the primary grades.* Portland, ME: Stenhouse Publishers.

Moffat, E. (2001). "Writing social stories to improve students' social understanding." *Good Autism Practice* 2 (1) 12-16.

Norris, C., & Dattilo, J. (1999). "Evaluating the effects of social story intervention on a young girl with autism." *Focus on Autism and Other Developmental Disabilities* 14, 180-186.

Rowe, C. (1999). "Do social stories benefit children with autism in mainstream primary school?" *British Journal of Special Education* 26 (1), 12-14.

Rust, J., & Smith, A. (2006). "How should the effectiveness of social stories to modify the behavior of children on the autism spectrum be tested? Lessons from the literature." *Autism: The International Journal of Research and Practice* 10, 125–138.

Sansosti, F.J., Powell-Smith, K.A., & Kincaid, D. (2004). "A research synthesis of social story interventions for children with autism spectrum disorders." *Focus on Autism and Other Developmental Disabilities* 19(4), 194–204.

Scattone, D., Wilczynski, S., Edwards, R. & Rabian, B. (2002). "Decreasing disruptive behaviors of children with autism using social stories." *Journal of Autism and Developmental Disorders* 32 (6) 535-543.

Smith, C. (2001a). "Using social stories to enhance behaviour in children with autistic spectrum difficulties." *Educational Psychology in Practice* 17, (4) 337-345.

Smith, C. (2001b). "Using social stories with children with autistic spectrum disorders: An evaluation." *Good Autism Practice* 2 (1) 16-25.

Swaggart, B. L., Gagnon, E., Bock, S.J., Earles, T.L., Quinn, C., Myles, B. S., & Simpson, R. L. (1995). "Using social stories to teach social and behavioural skills to children with autism." *Focus on Autistic Behaviour* 10, 1-16.

Wright, L.A. (2007). *Utilizing social stories to reduce problem behavior and increase pro-social behavior in young children with autism.* Unpublished doctoral dissertation, University of Missouri, Columbia.

About the Author

CAROL GRAY has over twenty-five years of experience educating students with autism. Carol initiated the use of Social Stories™ in 1991 and has written numerous articles, chapters, and books on the subject. Currently, Carol works privately with students, parents, and professionals in a variety of educational and vocational settings.

Every year, Carol gives many presentations and workshops throughout the world. She addresses topics related to the teaching of social understanding, bullying prevention, and friendship skills. Carol has received several awards for her work and international contributions to the education of individuals with autism and those who work on their behalf.

Here are some other helpful resources by Carol Gray!

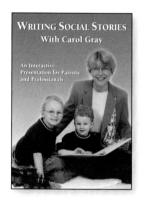

This DVD and accompanying workbook provide step-by-step training for writing effective Social Stories™.

ISBN 9781932565607 $34.95

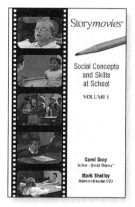

A Storymovie™ is a Social Story™ illustrated with a short movie. (Stories in this book that have corresponding Storymovies™ available have a "scene slate" icon near the Story number.)

Standard Edition: $89.95

Use simple drawings to illustrate interactions and explore social events, concepts, and skills with students.

ISBN 9781885477224 $9.95

Through the use of the Teacher Manual, Student Workbook, and an instructional DVD for teachers, this peer violence prevention program addresses bullying behaviors.

ISBN 9781932565447 $39.95

Extend teaching and learning with these great resources!

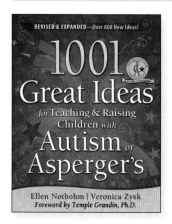

Winner of Learning Magazine's Teachers' Choice Award, this book presents parents and educators with try-it-now tips, eye-opening advice, and grassroots strategies.

ISBN 9781935274063 $24.95

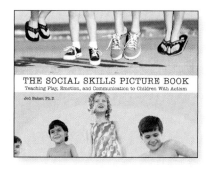

Winner of an iParenting Media Award, this book shows photos of students in real-life social situations, along with guidance on the right and wrong ways to react.

ISBN 9781885477910 $39.95

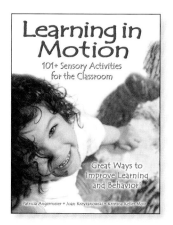

Ideal for preschool, kindergarten, and primary classes, each activity has been developed to attract and keep children's interest by using a multi-sensory approach.

ISBN 9781932565904 $24.95

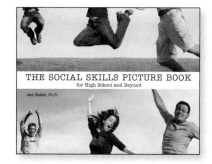

This picture book picks up where the first book left off, with social situations that teens and tweens will relate to. Winner of an iParenting Media Award!

ISBN 9781932565355 $39.95

Available at fine retailers everywhere!

These highly acclaimed books are great for parents!

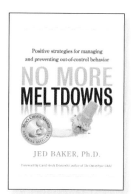
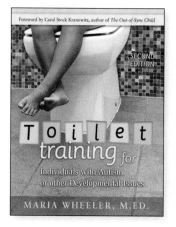
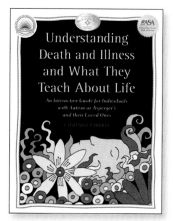